6-02

EU

THE FINAL WORLD EMPIRE

Alan Franklin

Printed in the United States of America

ISBN 1-57558-093-4

Table of Contents

Chapter 1

The Greatest Story Never Told

I'm in the news business, a professional journalist for thirty-eight years. Yet as I watch the TV news I realise that the truth behind the greatest story of our times is not being told.

Planes embed themselves into skyscrapers, germ terrorism is unleashed, and retaliatory missiles streak into the skies, while virtually all the Western media claims Islam is a "peaceful" religion. As thousands of victims of terror are buried, fanatical mobs march in a dozen Islamic capitals, burning effigies of President Bush and the British prime minister, Tony Blair. Yet both leaders suffer the delusion that if only "moderate Muslims" can be asked to assert themselves, the threats to the West will dissolve.

In the immediate aftermath of the New York and Washington terrorist attacks, churches had an attendance upsurge. But what was preached from the pulpits at what were often "interfaith" services? How many Americans—let alone Britons or other Europeans—were told that nations are often judged with enemy attack after God has removed His protection from them? How many preachers told their flocks to turn from their wicked ways, repent of their sins, and beg God for forgiveness?

Everything that happens in the world has a spiritual root. Perhaps the reason America was attacked in September 2001, was that it had turned away from God, murdered forty-three million babies in abortion clinics, and endorsed homosexuality, among other perversions of God's perfect way. As mosques were built all over the United States and false gods were worshiped everywhere, with horoscopes read more often than the Bible, could we honestly expect God to continue blessing us? The United States is the nation that has had more blessing than any since creation. Much is expected of those who have been abundantly blessed, and in too many churches false "feel-good" gospels and tales of acquiring riches through following "biblical" formulas have replaced the true Word of God.

So with our spiritual defences down, the way was open for our enemies to attack. Why do they hate America and Britain? Because America in particular supports Israel—the apple of God's eye. There are also more Jews in New York City than in any area outside Israel. And because Islam is inherently warlike and desires the destruction of all "infidels" (all those who do not subscribe to Islam) and "infidel nations." Osama Bin Laden and those who will follow him rightly divine that the West may have military strength, but its spiritual defences are weak, making it the perfect time to strike. If America can be given enough pain it may abandon Israel, the Muslims reason. Then they can move in to fulfill their number one aim: "to make the Mediterranean run red with the blood of the Jews." God, of course, has other plans. For as the earth is shaken and it becomes ever more obvious that we are moving into the biblical "end times," it is those who try to destroy God's chosen people who will themselves be destroyed, unlikely as this seems when you look at the map and see tiny Israel surrounded by a billion Muslims in more than fifty states.

With the new millennium just a few years old, many people think they have seen its darkest day. However, these terrible events were not a fulfillment of prophecy or the "fall of Babylon." The terrorism of 2001 was just a preview of wars and rumors of wars, death and destruction on a scale that will see up to three-quarters of the earth's population wiped out in battles and natural disasters, plagues and earthquakes, meteorite storms and tidal waves. The word "Titanic" conjures visions of a vast liner being sucked to the sea-bottom. The World Trade Center tragedy was like a fleet of Titanics going down. Imagine that multiplied by many millions and you will have some idea of what is in store in the near future.

Fortunately, God has told us exactly what is going to happen. Christians—and all who read this book—will have no doubt about how history will turn out. Finally, when all seems blackest and the final "Titanic" has settled beneath the waves, the world's armies will be gathered against Jerusalem. At that point, the Son of Man—the Lord Jesus Christ Himself—will emerge from heaven at the head of a mighty army, to retake and remake the world as it should have been from the creation.

Since September 11, 2001, people have been saying we live "in a changed world." In fact the same old fallen world chugs on as before, although the pace of change has gone up a gear. In particular, New World Order advocates like British prime minister Tony Blair have seized the chance to stress "globalised responses," to push harder for a world court, and to stress the importance of the United Nations—the putative one-world government in waiting.

As I write, TV news networks are talking of "panic," but I don't detect this, just a general, gloomy awareness of hidden threats. I see people who have been sedated by sport and alcohol, soap operas and comedies, having to come face to face with cataclysm. They are not laughing any longer. And the script won't change even if you switch channels.

The scene is fast being set for the coming Antichrist, the one-world dictator who will lead the world government. Cash will soon be abolished, a prime excuse being that this step is the only way we can stop money from flowing to terrorist groups. It will be replaced by a computer chip implanted in our foreheads or right hands—if we are not Christians. For this is the mark the Bible calls "the mark of the beast," and any Christians living at that terrible time will have to refuse it and be martyred, for it is Satan's own stamp of ownership. At this time 144,000 Jewish evangelists will be spreading the Christian gospel round the world.

In this book I will reveal the steps being taken to monitor and control every citizen of earth, with computer tracking of every transaction, interception of all e-mails and phone calls, and giant computer banks which could be programmed to weed out dissidents—those who won't acknowledge the "New World Order." Already, far-reaching electronic surveillance is taking place and it is boasted that satellite spy cameras can read headlines from one hundred miles high. Even as I wrote this, the firewall on my computer flashed up several warnings that it had intercepted attempts at penetrating our system.

I will show how major branches of Christianity and even all world religions are rapidly coming together to form the one-world spiritual body which will try to control all worship. The argument is that this will quell aggression based on religious differences. Attempts will soon be made to license all preachers and those who don't conform to the one-world church will be out of business or forced to meet secretly, as already happens in much of the world, where hundreds of Christian martyrs are being created every day, unreported by the world's press, which would rather champion the rights of perverts.

I will argue that Bible-based values have almost disappeared in the West, where traditional values and decency are deliberately scorned in taxpayer subsidised perverted art, where schools often do not teach history in any depth and where a world which hasn't learned from past mistakes is doomed to repeat them. Complacent Christians, obsessed with their homes and gardens, cars, holidays, and stockholdings, are in for many more rude shocks.

I will point to Jerusalem as the world's top news location of all time, ever more so now that multiple prophecies about its future are coming true before our eyes. Jerusalem, mentioned over eight hundred times in the Bible and not once in the Koran, is the only city which God regards as especially His, the place where He has put His name forever (2 Chron. 6:6; 33:7).

Revelation 3:12 and 21:2 show there will be a new Jerusalem, something which is not said about any of the other major cities of the world. There will be a heavenly Jerusalem (Heb. 12:22), but no heavenly New York, London, or Paris. Control of Jerusalem is the one problem which man will never resolve—because the protagonists who claim it are not looking at what God wants for His city.

We are told by the Lord to pray for the peace of Jerusalem, but this is a serious business, as peace will not come to that city until two-thirds of the Jews have been wiped out. All this is predicted in the Bible, but how often is it preached? Who now knows that one verse in every thirteen in the Bible refers in one way or another to the second coming of Jesus, according to evangelist Dwight L. Moody. The second advent is a central truth of Christianity.

The biggest problem of all is that the church no longer teaches prophecy, despite the fact that the Bible is almost one-third concerned with prophetic events. Prophecy is "divisive," I have been told. It is "too difficult to understand" so we are better off ignoring it. And it wasn't meant to be taken literally, was it? Never mind that all the prophecies of the Lord's first coming were precisely, literally fulfilled. Let's all relax and concentrate on that nice God of love and wealth creation. Let's praise the Lord and pray for a new car, as He wants to bless His people if we are faithful with our tithes.

Give-to-get, or name-it-and-claim-it, is the prevailing gospel of many churches in the new millennium, coupled with excessive "tolerance" which includes holding services for sodomites and having bishops like Michael Doe of Swindon, England, calling for the church to "modernise" by holding blessing services for homosexual couples!

Even in the wake of terror in America, the Church of England was concerned with topics like whether a "sex-change vicar" could resume his ministry as a "woman"! This being the C of E, the only answer was yes . . . The only thing such people *won't* tolerate is Bible Christianity—and that is the way the world is fast moving as we go into the first years of the new millennium.

But what does "millennium" mean? It refers to Christ's future thousand-year reign on earth. I believe that reign is soon to start, so you need to learn about it while there is still time. First, dramatic events are scheduled on God's prophetic timeline. I believe the next major event will be the Rapture of the saints, or believing Christians. The term "saints" has been perverted and misused; in fact, all Bible-believing Christians are saints. Christians have been looking forward to the Rapture for almost two thousand years. It could take place shortly. Fantasy or science fiction? No, this event is prophesied by the most reliable book in the world, the book whose ability to accurately predict events in immense detail, hundreds or even thousands of years in advance, marks it out as divinely inspired. It is the Bible, the book that has never been wrong about anything. No other so-called sacred book, not the Koran, not Hindu nor Buddhist literature, dares make predictions, as they would be shown to be false, the works of deluded men. Only the Bible is history written ahead of time. The events I am describing are the world's near future, coming true just as the Bible predicts.

The Rapture, described in 1 Thessalonians 4:13–18, sees Jesus coming back to earth's atmosphere, descending from heaven with a shout to call His people home. One amazing aspect of this incredible event is that all over the world the dead will rise from graves and caskets, followed by the living believers who will "meet the Lord in the air." This will be the most astonishing event in world history since Jesus rose from the dead. It could happen any day now, for no Bible prophecy has to be fulfilled beforehand. Yet hardly a church teaches on it, scarcely a Christian expects it, and the world goes its chaotic way, oblivious and uncaring of the shattering events about to befall it.

Here's what the Bible predicts will happen at the close of this present age:

- Millions to vanish from the earth. Jesus meets His saints, His true church, and their appearance is transformed in the twinkling of an eye. Remember, this will only be for people who believe in their hearts, who have been born again, who have spiritually come alive by believing in the Lord Jesus. All the nominal, worldly Christians and liberal teachers and preachers will be left behind, and most of the "established" church will still be on earth going through their rituals.
- After the true church, made up of all those who love Jesus, has been removed from the scene, all restraint is gone. With only the nominal, ecumenical, apostate church to give its feeble "guidance," the earth will become ever more lawless and godless.

- This could well start an economic meltdown as populations and governments panic and wild stories circulate about where the missing millions of people have gone.
- Russia and its allies, mainly Islamic countries, could seize the opportunity to launch a massive attack on Israel.
- In the chaos, as politicians search for answers and try to calm people down, world leaders, led by New World Order advocates, might use the uncertainty to usher in the long planned one-world government and one-world currency.
- All savings would be wiped out overnight as the new currency is introduced, much as happened in the Weimar Republic in Germany in the 1930s, which paved the way for Hitler—a prototype of Antichrist.

Just a few prophetic ministries give insights into the Rapture and the end of the church age that follows, the rise and fall of Antichrist, the seven-year Great Tribulation—the worst time in the history of the world—and the soon destruction of most of the world's population, cities, seas, and civilisations with plagues, meteor strikes, earthquakes, and huge hailstones. A blueprint for the end of the world? No, but the end of man's misrule of the world and the end of up to three-quarters of the present population of earth. No other generation has had the means to destroy all flesh and as Matthew says (Matt. 24:22): "And except those days should be shortened, there should no flesh be saved: but for the elect's sake those days shall be shortened." Consider, too, that no other generation has had the facility to control all buying or selling by computer marks, so the end-times "mark of the beast" could not have happened until recently.

I am indebted to men of God like the Rev. Dr. Noah Hutchings of Southwest Radio Church Ministries of Oklahoma City, and all the staff of this great prophetic ministry, who first kindled my interest in prophecy. And I thank God that, as a journalist with a great fascination for the pattern of world events and access to many sources of news, that I have been shown how these truly are the times of the signs, the times of the end, when the last great Bible prophecies will be fulfilled, culminating in the greatest event of all, the return of Jesus Christ, King of kings and Lord of lords, to finally defeat Satan, Antichrist, and the false prophet and their hundreds of millions of followers.

Hardly a day passes when I fail to detect some sign of the end of history—United Nations' meetings on world religion and world government, the increasing promotion of "one world" in school book days, environment days and so on, a call for a global currency. The breaking down of the nation state; the claim that nationality and pride in country is old-fashioned, that the future is in shared sovereignty: "Sovereignty pooled could be sovereignty renewed," as Britain's premier Tony Blair said in a particularly idiotic quote, about as meaningful as departing American president Bill Clinton shouting at his last Democratic convention as president: "Don't stop thinking about tomorrow." We are governed by men without deep insights, although my feeling is that our visible rulers are not really the ones pulling the strings at all.

In 1844 British prime minister Disraeli wrote this mysterious comment: "The world is governed by very different personages from what is imagined by those who are not behind the scenes." Nelson Rockefeller, believed by many to be the main financier of the New World Order, wrote in *The Future of Federalism* in 1962: "The nation state is becoming less and less competent to perform its international political tasks. These are some of the reasons pressing us to lead vigorously toward the true building of a new world order. Sooner perhaps than we realise there will evolve the basis for a federal structure of the free world."

Occasionally the hidden hands pulling our world into one huge global superstate, ruled by a powerful elite, are revealed. In particular the role that covert American operations have played in dragging Britain into the mire of Euroland has been shown in declassified American government documents. These reveal that the U.S. intelligence community ran a covert campaign in the 1950s and 1960s to push for a united Europe. It directed and funded the European federalist movement—and behind the scenes were the usual suspects from the Rockefeller and Ford Foundations, long controlled by "one-world" enthusiasts keen to abolish the nation state.

Incidentally, a report in the *Financial Times* of September 22, 2000, said that Belgian's prime minister, Guy Verhofstadt, had just called for the creation of a full-fledged European army "in the relatively short term." He has an ambitious plan for deepening EU integration. How the Euro army, set to be in place by 2003, will fit in with NATO is unclear, but many, from Lady Margaret Thatcher on down, think NATO can only be weakened by it.

The U.S. documents confirm fears voiced at the time that, behind the scenes, America was trying to push Britain into a United States of Europe. One memorandum of July 26, 1950, gives instructions for a campaign to promote a fully integrated European parliament, much as now exists in Brussels and Strasbourg, twin homes of the European superstate. This document is signed by General William J. Donovan, head of America's wartime Office of Strategic Services, forerunner of today's CIA. Belgian's premier says that a charter of fundamental "rights" currently being drawn up in Brussels can be a stepping stone to an EU constitution. Did those Americans realise how successful they would be, and the true nature of the monster they would help unleash on the world?

The astonishing documents were found by Joshua Paul, a researcher at Georgetown University in Washington and include files released from the U.S. National Archives. America used the American Committee for a United Europe, formed in 1948, to pursue its agenda. This committee was chaired by General Donovan. The vice-chairman was Allen Dulles, the director of the CIA in the fifties. On the board were the CIA's first director, Walter Bedell Smith, and people who had worked for the OSS and also the CIA.

The documents found by Mr. Paul show that the American Committee for a United Europe financed the European Movement, the most important federalist organisation in the post-war era. In one year, 1958, it provided 53.5 percent of the movement's funds. The European Youth Campaign, an offshoot of the European Movement, was wholly funded and controlled by Washington. The Belgian director, Baron Boel, received monthly payments in a special account, according to a report from Washington by Ambrose Evans-Pritchard of London's *Daily Telegraph*, who says that when the head of the European Movement, Joseph Retinger, bridled at this degree of American control and tried to raise funds in Europe he was quickly reprimanded.

Says Evans-Pritchard in a report headed: "Euro-federalists financed by U.S. spy chiefs": "The leaders of the European Movement—Retinger, the visionary Robert Schuman and the former Belgian prime minister Paul-Henri Spaak—were all treated as hired hands by their American sponsors." Interestingly, the pope has recently started the canonisation process for Schuman and two other fathers of the European Community, viewing them as "saints" and the whole process as "heaven sent." Via the conduit of the CIA and Rockefeller money, seemingly . . .

The role of the Americans was strictly covert and the funds came from the Rockefeller and Ford foundations and business groups with close ties to the U.S. government. The head of the Ford Foundation, ex-OSS officer Paul Hoffman, later doubled as head of ACUE in the late fifties. The State Department also played a role. A memo from the European section, dated June 11, 1965, advises the vice-president of the European Economic Community, (from the title of which the word "economic" was later stealthily dropped) to pursue monetary union by stealth. It recommends suppressing debate until the point at which "adoption of such proposals would become virtually inescapable." America also played a behind-the-scenes role in persuading the Danes to join the then European Economic Community.

The "great Danes" showed their independence in October 2000, however, by voting decisively not to join the Euro, thus throwing a Scandinavian spanner in the works of the "great project" and refusing to do what their press and media told them. They were immediately punished when their government raised interest rates, unnecessarily in the view of financial experts. In fact, it is the sickly euro which is constantly ailing and in need of support from the world's treasuries. In its first year it lost a quarter of its value against the dollar—what a great investment!

Other newly declassified American government files show that the U.S. tried to influence key figures in Denmark's political elite after the war, while funding and directing Euro federalist groups. The files reveal that Jens Otto Krag, the prime minister who took Denmark into what was then called the Common Market in 1972, was a guest of the Bilderberg Group. These are top political, newspaper, and industrial figures, including bankers and treasury mandarins, from Europe and America, who meet in secret to "guide" the future of the world. At that time the Bilderbergers were promoting European integration, which was also U.S. government policy, despite its seemingly obvious disadvantages for America.

It is particularly interesting that this tiny glimpse into the activities of the Bilderberg Group came to light as I was writing this book, for although they, and groups like the Trilateral Commission in America, are widely suspected of manipulating the world agenda, hard evidence is difficult to come by, although we know that many senior politicians are invited to Bilderberg meetings—men like Tony Blair, Britain's current prime minister. He claimed, in a speech made in Edinburgh, Scotland, as part of his successful 2001 re-election campaign, that it is somehow patriotic to get rid of your national currency—a real Alice in Wonderland view! Baroness Margaret Thatcher, Britain's doughty former prime minister, stated in June 2001 that Blair is a man committed to the extinction of the nation of Britain. Many of my friends in the Christian "end times" arena suspect the hand of shadowy organisations—and other secret societies—behind some world leaders and political movements and much of what happens in the world seemingly by accident. However, as a journalist I like to have proof.

Sometimes the shape of things to come casts a long shadow beforehand. For example, one former British army officer believes that Europe's future was decided in 1940. In a letter to the *Daily Telegraph* (London) which appeared on November 26, 1997, under the heading "Euro Visions," Graham Langmead, of Bognor Regis, West Sussex, England, wrote the following:

The first I heard of a common European currency was from [German] General Von Vietinghoff, to whom as a very junior officer I was escort at Bologna in April 1945, just after he surrendered the German forces in the central Mediterranean.

Apart from his outrage at being put in the charge of a 20 year old lieutenant, he let me know that a Franco–German agreement had taken place in 1940, just after Dunkirk and the splitting of France into "occupied" and "unoccupied" zones, and that Europe would become one state controlled by Germany and France regardless of what happened from then on. He boasted that Germany had obtained the agreement of France to run Europe after the war, regardless of the military outcome. "The French are our friends." He told me that there would be one currency which would create a European state under German dominance.

Of course this has now happened and in January 2002 the euro replaced national currencies in twelve European states.

Interestingly, in classical mythology Europa was a princess (of Phoenicia) and paintings of the woman on the beast usually depict the abduction of Europa by the Greek god Zeus, who disguised himself as a bull. There is a famous painting by Titian, "The Rape of Europa." Europe is indeed fast turning into the kingdom of the beast, as I reveal in the next chapter.

American readers will probably not have heard of him, but British, Australian, and New Zealand Christians may well know of Barry Smith, the New Zealand evangelist, author, and speaker. We were privileged to have Barry and his wife May stay with our family on a couple of occasions in the late 1980s when Barry was on speaking tours of Britain. Barry believed that one-world government was on its way and that, in Europe, the Bilderbergers were at least partly behind it.

Barry has been touring the world for over thirty years preaching that the end times described in Bible prophecy are coming soon, starting with a money crash followed by a one-world currency, a one-world government, and a one-world dictator—the Antichrist. Barry presented me with his book *Second Warning*, one of a series which he has published himself and which I recommend to anyone who wants a deep insight into the fast approaching world government and the secret forces behind it. The address of his agents is in my bibliography. Although Barry would be the first to admit he doesn't get everything right, and he does not claim to be a prophet, many events now coming to pass in the world were foreseen by Barry decades ago.

Barry has for years drawn attention to the following one-world government enthusiasts: the Council on Foreign Relations, a group which advises presidents on foreign policy; the Trilateral Commission, which encourages top level meetings on world government matters, and the Club of Rome, famous for churning out doom-laden and often wrong forecasts on the future of the world. One thing that Bible-believing Christians have in common with the Rome doomsters is a belief that the world cannot go on much longer in its present ways. There the similarity ends. The world government people believe the threat is posed by overpopulation, resources becoming scarce, pollution problems, and so forth.

We know that the world's essential problem is spiritual—for the most part, its six billion people follow false gods. Many years ago the Club of Rome divided the world into ten regions and today, in the new millennium, regionalisation is the new buzzword, with regions of countries replacing old historic counties in power and influence. World regions are also advocated by the World Federalists, whose detailed plans for world government I have obtained. Perhaps the rulers of the ten world regions are the ten "kings" ruled over by the Antichrist. It seems unlikely that they will be monarchs.

Alerted by Barry's talks and books, I decided to start investigating things for myself, and over the past fourteen years have amassed a huge amount of evidence, much of it coming to me by way of press releases from government or EU organisations which are happy to tell you of their plans—up to a point. When you have been alerted to the big picture, all the little jigsaw pieces fall quickly into place.

I have no secret information, just masses of corroborative news items which show clearly what is ahead, a stealthy, step by step process to take away our liberty, free speech, press, and political freedom—and give it to a world government which in turn will hand it over to the coming world dictator. Remember this every time you see words like "globalism," "global village," and "one world"; every time your children are invited by their schools to take part in "One-World Week," "World Book Day," and a host of other events which push the globalist agenda. The whole truth behind this mental softening up process never comes out, because the whole truth would be too terrifying a pill to swallow. Those who would subjugate

National culture is sublimated to a series of "world" themed events designed to weaken children's pride and make them "world citizens" of the coming one-world government.

the world must move one step at a time, denying everything if too much of the plan is revealed before the time is right. The roots of all this go back to the days of Cecil Rhodes and his plans for world domination, and further back still, to esoteric secret societies. It would seem fantastic—were not it all true.

This evil advance of the one world plan, involving every kind of double dealing and chicanery, is a process which has continued to this day. One blunder by the spin doctors of Europe was revealed when the European Commission's media service accidentally released a memo that called for "hypocrisy" and "evasion" to be used when dealing with the press. In other words, truth is what these people say it is at any given time. We live in deadly dangerous times, when truth is being stood on its head and used as a "tool." One British government spin doctor, just one hour after the attack on the Twin Towers in New York, sent out an e-mail memo stressing that now was a great time to release bad news, as nobody would notice! Readers, beware!

Jesus' disciples were curious about the signs of His return and of the end of the age. Here is what he told them: "For then shall be great tribulation, such as was not since the beginning of the world to this time, no, nor ever shall be. And except those days should be shortened, there should no flesh be saved: but for the elect's sake those days shall be shortened" (Matt. 24:21–22). In the Old Testament there are over three hundred references to Christ's comings, both first and second. In the last seventy-two hours of His life, thirty-three of these prophecies were literally fulfilled. The chances of this being a coincidence are one in 33,554,432. Still an atheist? If you are, God has this to say: "The fool hath said in his heart, There is no God" (Ps. 53:1).

There are many other signs that these are the end times, as distinct from all the other disasters, wars, and earthquakes the world has suffered since the fall. The main one, of course, is the restoration of the state of Israel in 1948. Here's what Ezekiel predicted over twenty-five hundred years before it took place: "And I will bring them out from the people, and gather them from the countries, and will bring them to their own land, and feed them upon the mountains of Israel by the rivers, and in all the inhabited places of the country" (Ezek. 34:13). All the end-time prophecies in the Bible have the Jews back in control of Jerusalem. The fact that these people were scattered, yet for two thousand years kept their language, culture, and religion and then regained their homeland, is one of the great miracles of history and testimony to the truth of Bible prophecy. The recapture of Jerusalem from Jordan in 1967 set the scene for the fulfilment of this prophecy.

Let's hear from Ezekiel again: "And they shall dwell in the land that I have given unto Jacob my servant, wherein your fathers have dwelt; and they shall dwell therein, even they, and their children, and their children's children for ever: and my servant David shall be their prince for ever." (Ezek 37:25)

The return of the Jews to their ancient home is one of the most amazing events of history, achieved immediately after Hitler had attempted to exterminate them and in the face of the hostility of the entire Arab and Islamic world and in spite of the difficulties posed by Great Britain, then administering Palestine under a UN mandate. There could be no greater proof of the authority of God

and the truth of His Word. No other ancient nation has survived
with its religion, practices, language, and ancient literature intact.
No other nation has been so persecuted, attacked, vilified, and dis-
persed round the globe, only to be miraculously regathered, then
to—again with divine intervention—survive an immediate attack
from the combined armies of six Arab nations. No other people
attract such hostility, something which I saw firsthand on a visit to
Tangier, Morocco, which is a long way from the Holy Land. A young
Arab boy was our guide round the ancient city. He was a pleasant,
cheerful lad, until he came upon the home of some Jews. He then
rushed up to their door and spat forcefully on it, pulling a face, and
shouting out "Jews."

Even now most of the world wants Israel abolished. Boutros
Boutros-Ghali, UN secretary-general, has stated: "The Jews must
give up their status as a nation and Israel as a state, and assimilate
as a community in the Arab world." Were they foolish enough to
try this, they would get a dusty welcome. This is what the Palestine
Liberation Organisation has to say about Israel: "The struggle with
the Zionist enemy is not a struggle about Israel's borders, but about
Israel's existence."

The PLO is an Islamic terror organisation which has trained
terrorists worldwide, from the Italian Red Brigades to Germany's
Baader-Meinhof gang, from Iran's Revolutionary Guards to Latin
American terrorists. The PLO has a history as one of the world's
worst terror organisations, at one time having hijacked four aircraft simultaneously and on another occasion holding three hundred hostage. They have attacked embassies, ships, diplomatic missions, and schoolchildren. The Palestinian prize for culture was
awarded for a book celebrating the murder of eleven Israeli ath-
letes at the 1972 Munich Olympics. Having been driven out of Jordan by the loyal Bedouins of the late King Hussein, the PLO established a reign of terror in Lebanon where they are estimated to
have murdered three hundred thousand Lebanese civilians. Yet
somehow the world classes the Israelis, who seek to protect themselves against these thugs, as the villains!

It was the Arabs who invited Pope John Paul to Bethlehem to

celebrate "our Jesus Christ." Arafat claims Jesus as an early Palestinian freedom fighter against Israel, in a weird perversion of true history. The man who has been involved with terrorism much of his life has now been given the Nobel Peace Prize and is received warmly by the pope on his visits to the Vatican. He has remodelled himself as a "moderate" and loves to be pictured with presidents at Camp David. But remember, at the time of the Gulf War his PLO gave its full backing to Saddam Hussein, mainly because of his plan to destroy Israel.

This was a miscalculation which led to the withdrawal of financial support from oil-rich states which previously employed hundreds of thousands of Palestinians as servants and low-level workers. After the war many of these Palestinians were thrown out of countries like Kuwait because their loyalty was suspect, increasing the pressure on the PLO to claim ever bigger chunks of Israel for their burgeoning population. Another miscalculation came when Palestinians were pictured celebrating in the streets after the 2001 attack on America—a glimpse of their true feelings before Arafat's spin doctors stepped in and said it was all a big mistake . . .

A London-based Islamic newspaper called *al-Khilafeh* said this about Jerusalem: "It is where the Creator informs us there is to be blessing—not to be polluted with the filth of the Jews in the city of al-Quds [Jerusalem]. It is to that city and to that land we look for the soon to come Islamic army to liberate." This would be the first stage of the world conquest by Islam in a *jihad* against Jews and Christians. An Islamic student questioned by the *Jerusalem Post* on August 3, 1996, said: "Our vision for the Middle East is that it is a centre for Islam, from where it will spread to the whole world sooner or later." Politicians' so-called peace plans, conducted from man's point of view, not God's, will never bring peace to the Middle East. In fact, the Bible says that it will not be peaceful until the Lord returns to conquer His enemies. Until then it will increasingly be the scene of conflict. No wonder our Lord wept over Jerusalem!

God is in charge of history, not politicians. He makes sure His prophecies are fulfilled. God has also promised to bless those who bless Israel and curse those who curse Israel. Britain made things very hard for Jewish refugees fleeing to Palestine, at one time infamously shelling a refugee ship after surrounding it with six destroyers. Almost immediately, the British Empire, which until then had controlled a quarter of the earth's peoples, fell apart with astonishing rapidity. The empire on which it was said the sun never set, as it was so extensive, was rapidly reduced to a handful of offshore islands. Coincidence? Perhaps, but God is not mocked.

I remember seeing a film from Russia in which God was depicted as a foolish old man, running round pathetically in impotent fury. A lot of good this did the Communist states! Now Communism is a bad joke and Christian revivals are taking place in areas like remote parts of the Ukraine. God is not mocked for long. . . . It is interesting that Islam, which fiercely states that God has no son, doesn't seem to feature in the end-times scenario and I think it likely that it will be destroyed before then, in the very near future. An attack on Israel by many Islamic states would certainly seal their fate. Israel has nuclear weapons.

Jesus said there would be signs just before His second coming. "And he spake to them a parable; Behold the fig tree [Israel], and all the trees; When they now shoot forth, ye see and know of your own selves that summer is now nigh at hand. So likewise ye, when ye see these things come to pass, know ye that the kingdom of God is nigh at hand. Verily I say unto you, This generation shall not pass away, till all be fulfilled" (Luke 21:29–32).

This generation dates, I believe, from 1948 when the state of Israel was established, which is why I believe this is the last generation before the second coming of Christ. This is why Satan is so active in the world today—because he knows his time is short. This is why his man on earth—the Antichrist—will soon be revealed and will shortly take control. At that time books such as this will be banned. Buy extra copies. Spread them around to your friends and churches; make this part of your ministry. This book, together with my video *End Times News: EU—Final World Empire* (two hours packed with facts about these times of prophecy being fulfilled) will, with other works like them, be one of the ways in which unsaved people, left lost and bewildered after the true Christians vanish, can discover the truth.

At that time no Christian ministry will be on the air, no Christian books will be published, and the Bible, as it was for many years under the sway of the Roman Catholic Church, may again become a banned book, open only to official "priests" to interpret according to their own agenda. Already there are indications of moves to limit what can be preached as torrents of "equality" legislation pour out of Brussels for enforcement across Europe. It is little known that Article 51 of the EU Charter states that fundamental rights can be suppressed "if it is necessary and genuinely meets objectives of general interest being pursued by the Union." Human rights are unlikely to extend for long to those of us who oppose the creation of a superchurch—or "great whore church" as the Bible so pithily calls it. As I write, proposed new laws in Britain, supposedly aimed at restricting incitement to religious hate crimes, look likely to restrict any criticism of false religions.

Many one-world–minded news organisations already voluntarily suppress the truth. Tony Pearce, director of the Messianic Testimony and publisher of the end times newsletter *Light for the Last Days*, wrote this in the Spring 2000 edition, under the heading "Government control of the media—how safe is our democracy?":

> An area of concern such [one world] groups have is how to manage popular opinion through the media. At a meeting of the Trilateral Commission in 1991, its founder, David Rockefeller, said: "We are grateful to the *Washington Post*, the *New York Times*, *Time* magazine and other great publications whose directors have attended our meetings and respected their promises of discretion for almost 40 years. It would not have been possible for us to develop our plan for the world if we had been subject to the bright lights of publicity during those years."

I met a Baptist whose mission field was in France. He was forbidden to place an advertisement about his church meetings in three local newspapers, on the grounds that his church was a "cult." In the end he had to distribute flyers door to door. Britain's Evangelical Alliance has noted that evangelical Christians are perceived by the EU as a sect and MEP David Hallam says that a European resolution on sects and cults permits the fast-growing European police force, Europol, to carry out surveillance on such groups. This armed force will soon be operating across borders and be responsible to the politically appointed judges of Strasbourg, operating outside national law. It is already collecting intelligence files on people, even those of us without criminal records! This police force, working with an EU public prosecutor, will itself have immunity from prosecution, by the way—yet another reason why many of us feel the superstate is already becoming quite sinister in nature.

On October 7, 2000, Ambrose Evans-Pritchard reported in his *Daily Telegraph* Eurofile column that EU ministers had agreed to extend the powers of Europol, the European police office. He said that Europol will soon be able to investigate money-laundering stemming from all forms of crime. He points out that this will create an open-ended mandate, since most crime involves the handling of money at some stage. In fact, it seems Europol itself may have already become too keen on handling money, for in June 2001, the Dutch criminal authorities said that the European Union's top police agency was itself under investigation—for alleged fraud and money laundering!

A report in the *Times* of London, published on June 16, 2000, was headed: "EU plans its own police force." The report stated that hundreds of British police would play a key role in a new Europe-wide civil disorder squad being planned by EU states. The plan is that the force will run in parallel with the military rapid reaction force currently being developed. Said the *Times:* "Under the proposals EU states would contribute police officers with specialist skills into a 5,000-strong pan-European force. Under the proposed force, special multinational units would be sent to uphold the law under the auspices of the EU, rather than by a member state government." This is very clever and follows the old Roman principle of never deploying the Roman legions to the country where they were recruited. That way there are no divided loyalties. For example, as I write the spearhead of the British Army is deployed in Kosovo.

On a visit to Strasbourg I was shown the French riot police, permanently deployed with their vehicles a few hundred yards from the EU parliament building. An EU minder recounted with glee how, when French peasant farmers were protesting at the building against the loss of their livings, they were brutally ambushed by this ruthless force, armed with steel-tipped wooden clubs, CS gas, and every kind of modern police attack weapon. I suspect that the first deployment of such a force into Britain will come as something of a shock, as we are used to a mainly unarmed, mainly friendly force of "Bobbies" who are, broadly speaking, on the side of the citizen. I am also intrigued as to where all these extra policemen are coming from, as all the police forces in Britain have mounted major recruitment drives to solve significant manpower shortages. Apparently, Europe can have what it wants of our scarce resources. The new supranational force will enforce one-world politics and one-world religion.

Fundamentalists' pulpits, the only places where the truth of God's Word is currently heard, will fall silent as the one-world church enforces its own version of spirituality. The liberal "caring" agenda will be prominent and we will also be urged to pray for the environment, to look after "Mother Earth," all the things that our selectively educated populations want to hear, brainwashed as they have been by the green agenda, or the big green lie machine, as I have called it. These deluded people are the enemies of God: I have a green activist's newsletter which ends with a salute to Gaia, the earth goddess.

What will the conditions be like just prior to our Lord's return? Let's look at eschatology, what the Bible's prophets foretell. Remember, as I said, unlike any other religious book, the Bible alone dares predict the future. In the Book of Revelation, the seventh and final letter to the churches is to the Laodicean church, the apostate, lukewarm church. It says, in part: "I know thy works, that thou art neither cold nor hot: I would thou wert cold or hot. So then because thou art lukewarm, and neither cold nor hot, I will spue thee out of my mouth" (Rev. 3:15–16).

Laodicea means "indifferent" or "lukewarm." The Holy Spirit is absent from this apostate church, just as He is absent from many churches in America and Britain today. Paul confirms in 2 Thessalonians 2:1–3 that before the day of the Lord comes men will be in danger of being beguiled and that when the "falling away" from the true gospel happens, the man of sin will be revealed, the "son of perdition" or Antichrist.

So in the closing years of the church age the Bible says it is inevitable that the church becomes apostate. Since the 1940s the liberal, ecumenical movement has grown greatly, preaching tolerance of everything except biblical fundamentals. Later in this book we will look at some of their acts and antics, from the bishop who says that being gay is like having ginger hair, to the vicars who bless the babies of homosexual couples. In the apostate church, ecumenism is the order of the day, with every town featuring an organisation called "churches together" holding joint activities and united promotions.

Some of the major denominations in Britain, particularly the Church of England, acknowledge the pope as the leader of Christianity, while all-things-to-all-people Alpha courses, a sort of nourishment-free fast-food Christianity, are held across most denominations. Catholics go through the course and emerge the other side still Catholics, despite the fact that many of the main Catholic doctrines go against the teachings of our Lord. Archbishop of Canterbury George Carey has been in regular unity talks with the pope and says he has "come to love and admire the Catholic Church." This is the church that for hundreds of years, until relatively recently, had the Bible on its list of banned books and whose priests are regularly charged with child abuse.

These have to be the end times; God will not for much longer put up with this vile rubbish. If Sodom and Gomorrah were destroyed, why should San Francisco be spared? These two ancient cities are a warning that God's Word is not vague or woolly in any way. God means what He says when He condemns homosexuality and today's so called "Christian homosexuals" should take note and change their wicked ways while there is yet time.

Before the vileness goes, the vilest man of all is set to appear: Antichrist. Hitler was a type of Antichrist, as was Alexander the Great. But their infamous deeds, and those of the wickedest men of history, will pale before what the final Antichrist, the Antichrist of Revelation, will do. He will try to counterfeit Christ, so will be part of an unholy trinity, with Satan the counterfeit father. There will be a false prophet playing the role of the Holy Spirit—this will possibly be the pope of the day, the leader of all the world's false religions rolled into one gigantic whore church, preaching blasphemies.

The false prophet will try to get people to worship Antichrist, the man described in Genesis 3:15 as the seed of Satan and in Revelation 11:7 as the beast. His other names in the Bible indicate aspects of his character, but we will call him Antichrist, which literally means "in place of Christ." Whereas Jesus was offered and declined the kingdoms of the world when He was tempted in the wilderness, Satan will offer his chosen one the kingdoms—and he will accept. This will be bad news for the world for a period of seven dreadful years, the seven years of the Great Tribulation, the worst time in the history of the world.

Who is Antichrist? He may well be on the earth today, waiting in the wings of the world scene for his moment of destiny. He will have Roman origins, according to Daniel 9:26–27:

> And after threescore and two weeks shall Messiah be cut off, but not for himself: and the people of the prince that shall come shall destroy the city and the sanctuary; and the end thereof shall be with a flood, and unto the end of the war desolations are determined. And he shall confirm the covenant with many for one week: and in the midst of the week he shall cause the sacrifice and the oblation to cease, and for the overspreading of abominations he shall make it desolate, even until the consummation, and that determined shall be poured upon the desolate.

The "he" in verse twenty-seven is the prince who is to come—Antichrist—and "the city" was destroyed by the Romans in A.D. 70, so that will be Antichrist's nationality. Incidentally, the founding document of the European Union is called the Treaty of Rome. The messianic Jewish Bible teacher Dr. Arnold Fruchtenbaum develops the theme of the origin of Antichrist, including his part supernatural origin, as he is spawned by Satan in person, in a booklet called *The Rise and Fall of Antichrist*. Publishers' addresses for this and other recommended books and ministries are in the index at the end of this book.

We also learn from Daniel 9:27 that Antichrist will be the man who signs a seven-year peace treaty with Israel, presumably on behalf of the European superstate which he will then be heading. This signals the start of the Tribulation. True Christians will not be here then; we will have been raptured prior to this event. There is no mention of the church in biblical accounts of the Tribulation. There are Tribulation saints, but these are people converted *after* the Rapture. The numeric value of Antichrist's name will add up to 666—the mark of the beast. Until this peace treaty is signed, the Tribulation cannot begin, so those who teach that we have somehow passed through it without noticing and are now in the thousand-year reign of Christ have some explaining to do. Incidentally, in the thousand-year reign Satan is bound, so if we are now in the millennium, as many teach, Satan must be on a pretty long chain!

Chapter 2

The Woman, the Beast, and the EU

People have been talking about the biblical "end times" for hundreds of years, so what is different about today and why do I think that world events are moving at dizzying speed towards the culmination of Bible prophecy?

I have been a journalist since 1964, spending ten years as a chief reporter and the last eighteen as the editor of a journal serving over two hundred thousand readers in southeast England. As a Christian versed in prophecy I cannot help but see in the emerging European superstate the foundations of a one-world government with a one-world dictator at its head—the man whose biblical names include the Beast, the Man of Sin, and Antichrist.

In fact, leaders in Europe are already calling for a strong leader, saying that committees do not work and they need more inspired leadership. German foreign minister Joschka Fischer repeated his call for a European superstate in July 2000, and said the European single currency—the euro—was "the first step to a federation." He added that he wanted a powerful president and the abolition of the Council of Ministers. He stated that the president—the "strong man" —could be selected with the "broad support" of the majority of member states with no veto. Speaking in Germany in 2000, he said his aim was "nothing less than a European parliament and a European government which really do exercise legal and executive power," to operate under its powerful president. But it gets worse—he also welcomed the progress made in removing the "sovereign rights" of nations which he said were the control of currency, along with internal and external security. Most of us would consider these rights a large part of our nationhood. Said Fischer: "Political union is the challenge for this generation." In the face of immediate terrorist threats, there are ever more urgent cries for countries to swap information, merge police forces, and work as one against the common enemy. All this brings the new world order much closer to reality.

Gerhard Schroeder, Germany's chancellor, called for the creation of a European government and a reformed and more powerful two-tier European parliament. His ideas were published in April 2001 in a draft party document proposing radical changes to the EU institutions. His Social Democrat Party, which is Socialist, confirmed that the plans, leaked to the German *Der Spiegel* magazine, were drawn up under his supervision. The basic idea is to replicate Germany's federal system of government at European level, reducing nation states to the standing of local regions. The Schroeder blueprint has a head or president of the European government. This man—a leading candidate for Antichrist at some future stage— would be elected, probably by the MEPs (members of the European Parliament) in the European Parliament. Back in 1970 leading financier Edmund de Rothschild said: "Western Europe is going to form a political union. The structure that has to disappear, the lock that has to be burst, is the nation."

The German Socialist scheme for a country called Europe was backed by the chancellor's party whose general secretary, Franz Munterefing, said in a report on May 1, 2001, that the proposals were to unite Europe within ten years. The party's blueprint said the single currency created new demands for harmonisation of economic policies and in particular taxation. The blueprint states ominously: "There is no alternative to further integration and Europeanisation." It also calls for Europol, the European police agency, to be turned into an operational European police vested with executive rights. This story was not regarded as unusual in Germany, where the whole process of creating a superstate meets little opposition.

Although there were grumbles when Germans gave up the

deutschmark, there has been almost no organised dissent and an official promoting awareness of Europe's new single currency in Germany was quoted as saying: "The most common question people asked was whether or not they would have to buy a new purse or wallet for their euros." For the euro to succeed, it will have to be backed by a strong government. Romano Prodi, the Italian who is president of the European Commission, said in May 2001 that the euro could fail unless the tax and spending policies of member states were brought under tighter EU control. He said the single currency would remain vulnerable as long as each country was able to run a separate budget policy in its own national interest. Watch out—that gurgling noise is your country disappearing down the plughole!

I was invited to Brussels, where the European Parliament is primarily situated, in my role as publisher of a business newspaper. I watched the vote taken as eleven countries abandoned their own currencies to form a united eurozone with the euro replacing everything from the lira of Italy to the Irish pound. They were effectively voting for the abolition of the nation state and it was astonishing to see with what little formality or protest countries like France and Germany gave up control of their financial and economic destiny to join in the project to create "a common European home," as the founding fathers of the European Union put it. No mention was made of the crippling cost to nations of scrapping their currencies. British accountants Chantrey Vellacott have worked out the figure for the U.K. alone as up to £32.8 billion! However, a committee of Westminster MPs (members of Parliament), chaired by Labor's Martin O'Neill, said the cost could be £35 billion and individual British companies with five thousand employees would have to find about £35.4 million each—money totally wasted and non-productive. The euro's introduction in note and coinage form was also widely predicted to be a great time for fraudsters and counterfeiters.

After the vote I went to lunch with six MEPS of different political parties. We talked about the future and I said that, as they now had one parliament and one currency, they were in many senses effectively one country. They could not really disagree, as the EU has all the trappings of a state, even its own embryonic army, the planned sixty thousand-strong rapid-reaction Eurocorps. So I asked: "Have any of you thought about the next step?" They asked me what I meant. So I explained that, with one currency, one parliament etc, the next big step was to have one leader, one fuhrer! After all, it was Hitler who was the last leader who tried to unify Europe under one government with one currency.

That many in Europe have been thinking on these lines for years is shown in a chilling quote from Paul-Henri Spaak, former Belgian prime minister and president of the Consultative Assembly of the Council of Europe nearly fifty years ago. He said:"We do not want another committee. We have too many already. What we want is a man of sufficient stature to hold the allegiance of all people, and to lift us out of the economic morass in which we are sinking. Send us such a man and, be he God or the devil, we will receive him."

More recently Jack Lang, then president of the French National Assembly's foreign affairs committee, in attacking the inertia of European foreign policy, said that Europe needed a strong central government with a single "personality" at the helm. Students of Bible prophecy will have little doubt who this "personality" will be. The present format of the EU cannot last and it was never intended that it should. Right from the beginning the founders had grand, globalist ambitions.

Addressing the European Policy Centre in September 2000, Belgian prime minister Guy Verhofstadt described the subterfuge adopted to set up the embryonic EU. "With the European Coal and Steel Community, the seeds were sown of the European Union of today. It was the initial impetus to the development of a community approach, step by step forging European integration by joining, and sometimes also by abolishing, national sovereignty into a joint approach." Turning to the next great leap forward, Verhofstadt says: "It is of the utmost importance to keep in mind a global vision of the ultimate goal of European unification." This is a good thing, he explains, because "the European Union as it is now could never be the ultimate goal." He says the pace of integration must never slacken lest "in the worst case countries will start to plead for the restoration of their former sovereignty." Notice that national sovereignty—independence—is referred to in the past tense.

Next comes a real bombshell. The Belgian says that there must be values underpinning this vast undertaking, the largest coming together of countries in the history of the world. But whose values? "In short, a Europe that attaches great importance to the values which result from the French Revolution." So the values of the brave new Europe are to be those of the country which gave us the guillotine, the Reign of Terror, and the time of blood washing through the streets of France.

The Portman Papers, a quarterly newsletter keeping watch on developments in the superstate, says in its October 2000 edition:

> Eight years before the French Revolution began in 1789 with the Declaration of the Rights of Man, the General Council of Freemasonry at Wilhelmsbad, convened by Adam Weishaupt, founder of the Illuminati, drew up the blueprint. Its evil spirit was epitomised in Maximilian Robespierre, whose technique anticipated Stalin's by 100 years.
>
> His master plan was to transform France into a Socialist state where absolute equality would prevail. But the population of France, 25 million, was too large to carry out his ideal. A plan of systematic depopulation was then decided upon. Conceived by the Jacobins, political intellectuals who sneered at "the stupid people of France" with their "souls of mud," the Reign of Terror claimed over a million victims. Inmates of prisons were slaughtered. Mass drownings in the dark waters of the Loire were organised, known as the noyades of Nantes. Human heads were counted up like scores on cards. The terror was justified in the name of "democracy."

Similarly the coming clampdown on frce speech, religious freedom, and free political parties by the "beast of Brussels" system is being justified by words like "anti-discrimination" and a "charter of rights." Human rights can easily become political wrongs . . .

Rules that came into force in Britain in February 2001 say that any group wishing to put up candidates for local or national government or the European Parliament must first be registered as a political party, which means red tape and cost. Here's the sting. Parties will not be registered unless their "financial structure" has been approved by the EU Commission. Donations are to be regulated and overseas contributions generally forbidden. If you or your donors are not approved by the EU, you are out of business. Goodbye, UK Independence Party? An electoral commission will rule on elections, referendums, and campaigning groups. Independent MP Martin Bell called the new act, rushed through Parliament under a device known as a guillotine to curb debate, "profoundly undemocratic." The police state is taking shape. The octopus is tightening its grip. The fast expanding Euro police force, Europol, could soon be used as the enforcement arm of the EU. Even the European Parliament's own report into this little known organisation said it could turn into "a repressive monster." Even worse, Europol staff have immunity from prosecution, something that even the royal family is denied.

Since its launch, the euro has floated like a stone. Being a currency of a federation that comprises both strong and weak economies, it is unlikely to be strong unless a United States of Europe is established. By early 2001 a majority of voters in several key Eurozone countries had turned against the wilting currency, with backing in Germany falling from forty-seven percent to twenty-nine percent in eighteen months. Unfortunately there were no political parties for these discontented folk to turn to. The money markets too have quickly worked out that a currency cannot work if there is no unity behind it—just a group of countries. So very quickly the twelve nations that make up the Eurozone, Greece having joined in January 2001, will have to give up their limited fiscal independence and submit to having their affairs run by a European central government. An ominous headline in Britain's *Daily Telegraph* of April 26, 2001, said: "EU tells Brown to curb spending." Gordon Brown is the British government's chancellor, in charge of spending and taxation. Note that the EU was "telling" him, not asking him. Money matters usually get the attention of governments, so expect the superstate to be on fast-forward.

Those countries that have had reservations about merging their currencies, such as France and Denmark, are told to keep holding referendums until the result comes out "right." France had turned the euro down once, so had to vote again, as this was politically unacceptable. On the second vote the result was too close to call, until there was a late arrival of ballot boxes from odd outposts of the French Empire, little offshore islands whose ballot boxes, oddly enough, were stuffed with "oui" votes. Denmark has had five referendums since joining the EU, with vast amounts of EU money being channelled so that the government-supported "yes" campaigns won four.

They slipped up on the fifth, the first Maastricht referendum, but were charmed into changing their minds by securing an opt-out from the single currency. Then, in September 2000, the Euro-federalists returned to try to take their currency away, armed with limitless money used for publicity to persuade them to drop the healthy krone for the sickly euro. All the volunteers who fought the "no" campaign had to raise their own cash, and were outspent twenty-three to one by the official government propaganda machine. Those MEPs like conservative David Hannan, who went over to help the "no" campaign, had witch-hunting liberals snapping at their heels, claiming they were using money for unlawful purposes. They weren't. They were fighting against a growing tyranny. And they won, at least for now.

This little country on the edge of Europe voted by 53.1 percent to 46.9 percent to keep its own currency, on a record turnout of 86 percent of the four million eligible voters. This was the biggest blow yet to the ailing euro, launched twenty months before. The Danes were rightly worried that their national sovereignty was being eroded, as it was and still is. Britain already has a big majority against the euro and the Socialist government there does not currently dare to call a referendum on the issue, as has been promised. The Danish vote shows that ordinary people can still make a dent in the Euro-machine, which threw all it had into this contest.

Every single part of the establishment, the political parties, the trade unions, newspapers, TV stations, and big business all told the Danes they "must" vote to integrate into the euro. Yet the ordinary people, barred from the mass media, as there is no hope of getting a fair hearing for anti-federalist views in most of Europe's journals, triumphed in the end. They did so because they believe in their country and its ability to govern itself. And in the end they refused to let Big Brother tell them what to do. This result makes it almost certain that Sweden, which is also outside the euro, will stay outside. Pia Kjaersgaard, who led the campaign against giving up the Danish krone, said after the result: "We have been given the opportunity to vote for our future and we have taken it. It means we will not be handing it over to unaccountable, unelected bureaucrats in Brussels." She called on the citizens of every other EU country to demand referendums of their own to express their disdain for the europhilia of the ruling elite.

An interesting question as yet unanswered is: what happens if a state, perhaps a little state like Ireland, refuses to obey a European dictat? This question may soon be answered. Charlie McCreevy, finance minister of Ireland, is refusing to comply with EU Commission requests for a suspension of tax cuts in the Irish budget. Says Charlie, quoted in February 2001 in the *Daily Telegraph:* "No country inside the Euro zone has given up the prerogative to run its own budget." The Commission has accused Ireland of banking up inflation and has invoked a treaty article that, says the *Telegraph*'s Ambrose Evans-Pritchard, "talks menacingly about the European Union's right to protect its collective interest." Watch out for the tanks on your lawn, Charlie! More likely, at this stage at least, when the menace behind the EU is largely hidden, a quiet behind-the-scenes plot will either remove Ireland's independent money-man or ensure that his policy changes.

In the summer of 2001 Ireland voted against the ratification of the Nice Treaty, which should mean that the whole process of further federalism is derailed. If even one EU member refuses to ratify the treaty, it is supposedly invalid. Immediately the result was announced, the rest of the EU said it was going ahead anyway—so much for popular opinion and the rights of the electorate. Watch for the frighteners to be put on and the next vote to be rigged, for nothing stops the EU juggernaut. Sure enough, after a few days came the expected reaction as EU foreign ministers ruled out any changes to the Nice Treaty and told the Irish government to find its own way out of its constitutional impasse. According to a report in the *Daily Telegraph* of June 12, 2001: "Given the Irish legal requirement that all constitutional changes should be approved by a referendum, the communique amounts to a demand that Ireland should have a second vote on the same substantive treaty text." In other words, vote again and get it right next time.

Remember how fast Maggie Thatcher went when she really started to stand up to the EU? Britain now has regular interference in our internal affairs, even down to the banning of a plan to cut Value Added Tax from 17.5 to 5 percent on church repairs. The Euro Commission says Britain's chancellor is not allowed to cut taxes on places of worship—and only a unanimous decision by EU finance ministers could change the law.

In January 2001 a poll carried out by eight leading European newspapers was published and showed dissatisfaction among voters extending across Europe, into all areas of European integration. Some seventy-two percent of German voters said they had little or no confidence in the ability of the European Commission to improve their lives, while in Spain approval of the commission was down to thirty-seven percent. In Britain, Europe's leading sceptic country did not disappoint, with sixty-two percent of voters backing the government's decision to keep out of the launch of the euro. However, not much of the future of the European project will be subject to democratic votes. Having seen how they can go wrong, from their point of view, the Brussels beast will ensure it doesn't happen again.

What is emerging in Europe is a Holy European Empire, an attempt to rebuild the old empire united under the pope. This is becoming increasingly blatant: The stained glass window of the Council of Europe at Strasbourg Cathedral features the Virgin Mary under a halo of twelve stars, the same stars you see on the EU flag. The Vatican is playing a major role in the creation of a new Holy European Empire and Catholic social values, so-called "Christian Socialism," are at its heart. Ever since the Reformation, the aim of successive popes has been to destroy protestantism in Britain and the present pope has repeatedly called for religious unity in Europe. This means a united Catholic Europe, which was consecrated to Mary by the Vatican in 1309. An interesting headline appeared over an article in the *London Times* on January 11, 2000: "It's impossible to be both a good Englishman and a good Catholic."

An insight into Catholic thought comes from an article by Stuart Reid, who is managing editor of *The Spectator*, a right-wing news and comment magazine. He wrote:

> Catholics still have a duty to distance themselves from the Protestant succession [to the throne of the United Kingdom] and all it stands for; indeed to pray for its failure. The nationalisation of the church, known to schoolboys as the Reformation, began a process that left Catholics divided in their loyalties. Since the fall of James II and the triumph here of German Protestantism, it has not been possible to be both a good Englishman and a good Catholic.
>
> When I was a boy we used to say a Prayer for the Conversion of England at Benediction (indulgence: 300 days; plenary once a month). It is not widely used these days, because it is considered poor form to talk of converting people, but it will resonate with any Catholic over 40. Cherie Blair [Catholic wife of the prime minister] will surely remember it with a trembling lip: "O blessed Virgin Mary, Mother of God and our most gentle Queen and Mother, look down with mercy upon England thy dowry and upon us all who greatly hope and trust in thee. . . . Intercede for our separated brethren, that with us in the one true fold they may be united to the Chief Shepherd, the Vicar of thy Son."

We cannot say we haven't been warned. Cherie Blair, is, of course, not only the wife of Britain's current prime minister, whose children are being raised as Catholics, but a leading barrister in

The Roman Catholic Church has always aimed for a united Catholic Europe. This Catholic map from 1592 shows Europe formed into the shape of "Mary."

London's law courts where she frequently pursues landmark cases in civil rights areas and "equality" laws.

Many are now campaigning for a repeal of the Act of Settlement which in 1688 barred Catholics from the throne of Great Britain. Yet the reason the throne is still barred to them is that the revolutionaries of 1688 rightly believed that Catholic teaching was false and against the Word of God.

When I visited Strasbourg, the French city near the German border which, with Brussels, co-hosts the European Parliament, I was introduced to the head of the house of Habsburg, Otto von Habsburg, the continent's leading lay Catholic and a man whose family dominated Europe for centuries. Full of charm and intelligence, he said that instead of war, a great new Europe could be built on peaceful cooperation. His ideas go far beyond this, however. In *The Social Order of Tomorrow*, he writes:

> Now we do possess a European symbol which belongs to all nations equally. This is the crown of the Holy Roman Empire, which embodies the tradition of Charlemagne, the ruler of a united occident. . . . The Crown represents not merely the sovereignty of the monarch, but also the ties between authority and the people. True, it is the monarch who is crowned, but in this sacred act he appears as the representative of the whole people. It should therefore be considered whether the European head of state, as the protector of European law and justice, should not also become the guardian of a symbol which, more than any other, represents the sovereignty of the European community.

Dr. Habsburg wants to see Europe have an elected head of state, a man elected for life. This influence of both Charlemagne and the Habsburgs hangs heavily over the new federal Europe. Back in

1978 the leaders of France and Germany made a pilgrimage to the throne of Charlemagne at Aachen. Afterwards, as reported by ex-leading EU civil servant Bernard Connolly, in his brilliant book *The Rotten Heart of Europe*, French president Giscard d'Estaing said: "Perhaps when we discussed monetary problems the spirit of Charlemagne brooded over us." Connolly was sacked for his honesty and lost his five-year battle against unfair dismissal in a ruling by the European Court of Justice on March 6, 2001. He said the court "is acting as the sinister organ of a tyranny in the making." This court has ruled that the EU can suppress criticism to protect its reputation.

This crown of Charlemagne, the first person to attempt to revive the Roman Empire in A.D. 800, is an inspiration to those who promote the breaking down of nation states, and a Charlemagne prize has been established for those who work hardest for European unity. One who does is ex-president Bill Clinton, who in June 2000, was the first American president to receive the Charlemagne prize for his work on promoting European unity. He received the prize at the cathedral in Aachen, Germany, where the first Holy Roman emperor lies buried. Clinton called for an enlargement of the EU, to take in even Russia.

A keen supporter of EU expansion. Why, I wonder?

In a report in the *Daily Telegraph*, London, of June 3, 2000, former president Clinton said the European Union should have at least thirty member states, including all the nations of the Balkans, Turkey, and possibly Russia. He said European peace and prosperity now depended on the EU setting its boundaries ever wider. The report stated that Mr. Clinton was determined to be viewed as "part of a family of statesmen associated with European integration." He held private talks with Helmut Kohl, the former German chancellor, in Berlin. Russia is currently working closely with the West against Islamic militants and an intriguing new line-up of countries looks possible.

Although Mr. Kohl has been discredited by a party funding scandal inside the Christian Democrat Union Party, and was central to Germany's worst post-war political scandal, he is still regarded as the most important force behind European integration in the past thirty years. In March 2001 he agreed to pay a fine of £100,000 after he admitted accepting political donations of £600,000 that were not declared in party accounts. The donors were never named, creating the suspicion that cash changed hands for favors.

It is easy to see how he and Clinton had much in common, but it is difficult to see how the establishment of a major, often anti-American power bloc in Europe could be in America's interests and surprising that it has been American policy to push for greater unification of Europe. It remains to be seen whether the second Bush administration, which seems to have some commonsense, sees the folly of creating a rival superpower in Europe which is anti-American and a threat to NATO. Here is what Baroness Thatcher, Britain's greatest prime minister since Churchill, wrote in the *Daily Telegraph* of June 1, 2001: "The European Army . . . conceived and driven by the French, as an alternative to NATO."

A few days after those words appeared in print, I was able to congratulate Lady Thatcher personally on her article when she visited Aldershot, known as the home of the British Army because of all its army training bases. She made a robust speech which my wife Pat reported and which I used as the front page lead in the newspaper I edit. The essence was that in this century, the world's main troubles have come out of continental Europe. The solutions have come from the English-speaking peoples, united against evil.

My wife Pat, who contributed the last chapter to this book, meets Lady Thatcher on a visit to Aldershot during the 1997 election campaign.

I was at a business conference in the late 1990s where the main speaker was a very senior American statesman. Afterwards we met and talked and I ended up driving him to the railway station and spending some time discussing the politics of Europe and how this affected America. I cannot name this man because at the time of writing he is still in office. However, when I asked him what the major problem for America was in Europe, he answered: "The French." It seemed that whenever the USA had a diplomatic or political initiative, the French would go out of their way to put their spoke in it. This is caused in part by their intense dislike of the domination of the English language in world trade and politics, and their jealousy of the Anglo-American "special relationship," which they are dedicated to breaking up. This is a main driving force behind their desire to suck Britain into the EU superstate, thus forcing it to give up its seats at "high table," on the UN Security Council, for example, where it has been a staunch ally of America since the UN was founded.

In an astonishing joint letter to the *Daily Telegraph* on June 12, 2001, eleven British and French generals warned that plans for a Euro army would not only damage both countries' armed forces, but could endanger world stability. They called the Euro army a "paper tiger" created by federalist politicians "playing at armchair generals" and said it would damage British and French national security. All eleven members of the group admit that French views on NATO's future are incompatible with those of Britain—and by inference America. The senior officers include Admiral of the Fleet Lord Hill Norton, formerly chairman of the Military Committee of NATO, and General Sir John Akehurst, a former Deputy Supreme Allied Commander, Europe. The French contingent was equally impressive and included Gen. Pierre-Marie Gallois, known as the father of the French independent nuclear deterrent doctrine.

As the amazing U.S. presidential election of 2000 was being fought to a dead heat, U.S. analyst Paul Craig was looking across the Atlantic and declaring that Washington should be worried about keeping London onside. He said Britain should be asked into the North American Free Trade Area to stop it being "sucked into" the EU single currency and, ultimately, a European federal state. Writing in *Investors' Business Daily*, he noted: "Once Britain is part of a European superstate, the U.S. will have lost its most important ally." For example, Brussels is bidding to take over Britain's embassies, with a gradual merging of British, French, and German embassies into an EU foreign service. There are also proposals for what is called "coordinated representation" on international bodies. This would mean, for example, the loss of Britain's seats on the UN Security Council, the International Monetary Fund, and the World Bank. So goodbye to three votes that almost always support American policy. An EU foreign service strongly influenced by the French would surely be a nightmare for US diplomats.

The anti-Europe publication *Facts, Figures and Phantasies* (September 2000) agrees, pointing out that traditionally Britain has relied on its NATO partnership with America for its defence, as has the rest of western Europe since the war. The newsletter reports that after British prime minister Blair met French president Chirac in 1998 he dropped previous British objections to creating a European defence structure, which had previously been said to threaten NATO. "The French got what they have always wanted, a structure shutting out the USA," commented editor Christina Speight. Britain's then Conservative Shadow Defence Secretary Iain Duncan Smith MP (now the leader of the Conservative Party) said:

> The French government has got what it required. All the documents signed at Nice make it absolutely clear that the European defence force is autonomous from NATO. It will not have to use NATO assets, but will only do if it decides to.
>
> Once an operation is conducted by the EU force, full political and military control will rest with the European Union, not with NATO, and EU military staff will also have a planning cell which will be capable of low level planning operations. . . . NATO does not have a right of refusal over EU operations, but in the document signed it is clear that the EU will make the decisions about operations first and not NATO.

Further details of the Conservatives' attempt to flush out the truth about the EU army can be found on their website, *www.conserva-tives.com*.

Meanwhile, the head of the EU's new military staff, Major-General Graham Messervy-Whiting, said the new rapid reaction force would start to compete with NATO once it acquired a full range of strategic military assets. The British general, speaking at a seminar at the Centre for European Policy Studies in Brussels, said that while humanitarian tasks would come first, in due course the new force would progress to operations like those of NATO in Bosnia.

The EU force is designed for deployment for up to a year, within sixty days, anywhere in the world, backed by four hundred aircraft, including seventy-two from Britain, and a naval force including eighteen major warships of the Royal Navy. Once rotation of forces is taken into account, this commitment would involve up to a quarter of a million soldiers, sailors, and airmen. It will be fully operational by 2003. What is being created is not just a European "rapid reaction force" to sort out the world's trouble spots now, but a force which can contain unrest *within* Europe when the Antichrist's empire is being built. Here's what French prime minister Lionel Jospin said on July 5, 2000: "By pooling its armies Europe will be able to maintain *internal* security and to help prevent conflicts throughout the world. If we manage to achieve this in 2000, we will have crossed a milestone towards the creation of a united, political Europe." Quite how you "cross" a milestone Monsieur Jospin doesn't explain . . .

Another enthusiast for the European superstate is Britain's prime minister Tony Blair, who matches ex-president Clinton in having a lawyer wife on the political left, frequently fighting court cases advocating political correctness. Blair, too, won the Charlemagne prize for his outstanding contribution to European unification. In his speech at the prize-giving he stated: "I want Britain to be at home with Europe because Britain is once again a leading player in Europe." However, the Britain he talks of is not one that historians of the past would recognise, but a Britain shorn of its statehood, independence, and freedom of action—a mere province of Europe, with a similar status there to that of, say, Missouri in the

USA. So just what is this new Europe Mr. Blair is taking us into, this premier who weekly attends Catholic church services?

The European flag consists of twelve stars, inspired by the halo of twelve stars around pictures of the Madonna. In the prayer room at Brussels Airport, gateway to the main EU capital, stands a statue of the Madonna, surrounded by the stars of Europe. A former sec-

Europe's flag—the stars of the Madonna.

retary general of the council of Europe, Leon Marchal, said the stars were those of "The Woman of the Apocalypse." The EU, which now has fifteen member countries, has confirmed that the number of stars will always stay at twelve, which indicates that the stars do not represent countries. I quote from a leaflet, "Building Europe Together," which I was given on a visit to EU headquarters in Brussels in 1998: "The European flag [is] a shared flag, blue with twelve gold stars symbolising completeness. The number will remain twelve no matter how many countries there are in the European Union." How odd this must strike Americans, whose flag proudly sported a new star as each fledgling state came into the union.

The same document, issued to commemorate "Europe Day, May 9," also boosts Europe's new common anthem, "Ode to Joy," the

May 9 is supposed to be celebrated across the continent as "Europe Day."

prelude to the last movement of Beethoven's Ninth Symphony. The EU document states: "Officially the Ode to Joy, but which in this context also means the ode to freedom, to a sense of community and to peace between the fifteen countries which have decided to unite and to others which will freely decide to join them." In fact the "Ode to Joy" is not quite that innocent, as the lyrics, by a man called Schiller, concern the entering of the shrine of a pagan goddess and the uniting of all men in brotherhood, by the power of magic, according to Adrian Hilton in *The Principality and Power of Europe*.

An amazing poster was issued by the European Union, showing the Tower of Babel and carrying the slogan: "Many tongues, one voice." This appears to be an attempt to reverse God's judgment on Babel. In case the point was lost, a crane in the back-

ground was shown rebuilding the tower. Above the Tower of Babel were shown the eurostars, but inverted and shaped like pentagrams, as in witchcraft, with the central points downwards. Nimrod and his followers tried to build a tower to reach the heavens, but it was the counterfeit building of a counterfeit religion. In those days stone was commonly used for buildings, but in the Tower of Babel bricks were used—man-made objects as opposed to God-made. The Babylonian "queen of heaven" was the mother of Nimrod. Today it is what Roman Catholics call Mary, mother of Jesus.

A European Union poster depicting the Tower of Babel being rebuilt.

The story of the rise and fall of Babylon told in Genesis chapter eleven should have been a warning to all men for all time. Nimrod's tower of staggering height was intended to serve religious purposes, for it is thought to have honored deities in the heavens. Mystical Babylon is now being rebuilt in Europe, and although they don't speak each other's languages, this is not stopping those behind this incredible, evil project.

Pieter Brueghel's representation of the Tower of Babel.

At present the EU works in eleven languages, necessitating fifty-five separate translation combinations. Once countries like Poland and Hungary and other candidate nations are admitted, the translation combinations could rise to one hundred and twenty for every document and speech. There are currently nineteen hundred translators, a number set to explode. Imagine trying to find a Spanish or Greek speaker prepared to sit in the glass translators' boxes turning politicians' waffle into Finnish—or Portuguese? Only an idea from hell could create so much confusion.

Those who would follow Nimrod have now succeeded in building a vast new headquarters in Strasbourg, France. Astonishingly, its centrepiece is an enormous replica of the unfinished Tower of Babel. Babel's original meaning was "gate to God," but Nimrod founded an idolatrous religious system in which people were expected to worship the images he set up. He also brought in a political dictatorship and his tower was a symbol of one man's revolt and desire to make a name for himself. If you have a powerful, one-world leader in rebellion against God, you have a formula for world dictatorship. The choice is between Bible—or Babel.

Even the secular press could not miss the connection between the old and new towers of Babel and labelled the new French structure "The Tower of Eurobabel." This vast edifice holds an auditorium equipped with seven hundred fifty seats, a strange number since the EU has set a ceiling of seven hundred seats for its MEPS (members of the European Parliament), even when it expands to take in countries to the east that were formerly part of the Russian Empire. I am told that nobody sits in seat number 666! This huge, monumental building, full of labyrinthine corridors, is used

New EU parliament building in Strasbourg, France. Note the unfinished "Tower of Babel" centrepiece. I wonder who will arrive and order its completion? Perhaps the occupant of seat 666, which remains empty!

only one week in four, because the rest of the time the EU Parliament meets in Brussels. Every three weeks the whole caboodle shuffles between the two sites in a fleet of two hundred trucks, at enormous expense. An MEP I know was there on the day Eurobabel opened and reported total chaos in the £300 million structure, commenting: "If they can't run a building, should we trust them with a continent?"

Nigel Farage is a member of the European Parliament who belongs to the United Kingdom Independence Party, which is fighting to get Britain out of the superstate. He said in an article just after the opening day: "We realise we are not merely entering a building, but being allowed access to the temple of a bold new empire." I know Nigel and he is a perceptive young politician, but his instant impression was more accurate than even he probably realised at the time. The building itself is designed to make the inhabitants feel humble, a monstrous pile of fourteen thousand tons of steel and one hundred forty thousand cubic yards of concrete.

Nigel said it resembled "the mother ship from *Close Encounters* descending on the gasometers next to The Oval" (a cricket ground near London, England). As for the debates, there is instantaneous translation into eleven languages—including one that Nigel says might be Martian. In the space of forty minutes on the opening day, MEPs were asked to vote by swipe card up to seventy times, and many of them said they had no idea what they were voting on. They didn't need to know, for all the big parties' MEPS were told what to do by their party bosses. Many of the MEPS, together representing three hundred seventy million citizens of Europe, are more interested in their perks, like chauffeur-driven limousines and expenses, than in the voting procedures. Such is democracy in the brave new world of the future Antichrist's empire.

Unusual biblical symbolism is starting to appear in Europe, which again tells a clear story to those of us who know what the Bible foretells. Britain issued a stamp to commemorate the European Parliament elections (each country directly elects its representatives to the assembly). The stamp depicted a woman riding the beast—Mystery Babylon the Great? I had an even greater shock as I flew over from Great Britain to record a series of programs for Southwest Radio Church Ministries and others. I picked up the United Airlines' magazine from the seat pocket, turned a page, and found the headline "Guten Morgen, Europa!"—good morning, Europe.

This is how the article started:

The cover of *Der Spiegel* magazine, showing the woman flying the EU flag.

This May, a daring picture appeared on the cover of *Der Spiegel*, one of Europe's most prestigious news magazines: a pitch black bull, horns lowered, charging straight at the reader. On its back sat a young woman draped in dark blue cloth and waving the blue flag of a united Europe. The cover was a delight for European readers since the woman was the very popular French supermodel Laetitia Casta, who had also recently been selected as the "Marianne 2000" in France—the feminine personification of the French Revolution. . . .

The writer imagines the bull refers to a period of business bullishness, but unfortunately he misses the point. There are paintings and statues of the woman and the beast appearing in official Brussels circles and also, reputedly, on a hastily withdrawn poster. A mural of the woman and the beast even decorates Brussels Airport lounge.

The woman on the beast is now the official picture of the EU, according to the Rev. Dr. Ian Paisley, the Northern

Illustrations of the woman and the beast are cropping up throughout the EU, particularly in official buildings.

Ireland Protestant minister and member of both the Westminster and European parliaments as well as the Northern Ireland Assembly. He said that when the multibillion dollar new parliament building in Brussels, Belgium, was completed, in the great glass house at the end where the parliament meets is a dome. On this dome is a colossal painting, three times life size, of the woman riding the beast. When Dr. Paisley tried to take a party of people to view this monstrosity he was told the room "is closed at the moment."

In Strasbourg, France, the rival new headquarters of the parliament features a building called PE1, the parliamentary offices. Here in the offices is a painting of a naked woman riding the beast. Dr. Paisley describes going into the office of a German parliamentary colleague and seeing a horrible print of the woman and the beast on his wall. The German MEP said that thousands were printed, but such a fuss was made about them in Germany that they were withdrawn. He had got hold of one, in the hope that it would rise in value as a collectors' item. When designs for the new euro coin were unveiled, sure enough, there was the woman riding the beast on the back of the Greek euro coin. In 1992 a German ECU coin was issued showing Europe and the beast.

In the new Brussels building of the Council of Europe is a bronze statue of the woman riding the beast, and the beast is depicted riding the waves. The woman and the beast were even shown on a stamp issued by the British Post Office to mark the elections to the European Parliament. Scripture is being fulfilled before our eyes, or for those with eyes to see. If many leaders in Europe have taken as their symbol the sign of the woman and the beast—Antichrist's woman symbolising the harlot church of the end times—it points to the rapid fulfilling of Scripture. Dr. Paisley said in an address, a tape recording of which I have, that a system of government dominated by the whore church is fast being prepared.

He was asked by a questioner what was behind all this, and did they know what they were doing. He said that it was always impossible to find the individual responsible, as these projects came out of the commission's secretariat (Europe's ruling body who propose new laws in secret). However, although ignorance of Bible prophecy can be assumed to be widespread in Europe, it occurs to me that there must be senior people who know what is going on. And above them are demonic spirits, and Satan himself, and they definitely know what they are doing. Not all secular people are entirely fooled, either, as I sometimes see headlines referring to "the Beast of Brussels," etc.

Interestingly, this term was allegedly used as long ago as 1976 to describe the enormous new computer constructed in Brussels to keep electronic watch on the citizens of the Eurostate. *Moody Monthly* magazine apparently picked up this astonishing news item: A senior Brussels analyst (name withheld by author)

announced today from Brussels that a computerized restoration plan is already underway in the aftermath of world chaos. In the crisis meeting, which brought together scientists, advisors and Common Market leaders, Dr. --- unveiled the "beast." The beast is a gigantic computer that takes up three floors at the administration building at Common Market headquarters. This monster is a self-programming unit that has over one hundred sensing input sources. Computer experts have been working on a plan to computerise all world trade. This master plan involves a digital numbering system for every human on earth. The computer would assign each citizen of the world a number to use for all buying and selling to avoid the problems of ordinary credit cards.

The number could be invisibly laser-tattooed on the forehead or back of the hand. It would provide a walking credit card system. The number would show up under infrared scanners to be placed at all checkout counters and places of business. Dr. --- suggested that by using three six-digital units, the entire world could be assigned a working credit card number. Other Common Market officials believe that the present chaos and disorder . . . point to the need of a world currency, perhaps an international mark that would do away with all currency and coin.

If true, this is an amazing statement, but I have not been able to authenticate this quote, which has been widely reprinted in Christian circles. The huge computer mentioned does exist, however, and is nicknamed the beast although its actual name is EuroNet.

Note the mention of a world currency in the quote above, because again I feel that many Americans are deluding themselves that troubles in Europe are safely far away. Do not be deceived. A Federal Europe is just step one in the plan for a New World Order. A Congress of Europe, meeting at The Hague, Holland, in 1948, adopted seven resolutions on political union. This is what resolution seven says: "The creation of a United Europe must be regarded as an essential step towards the creation of a united world."

I hope to go to EU headquarters again shortly to capture some of this on film, as it seems so amazing that I do not think Americans will believe it until they have seen it. However, everything I have mentioned I have personally seen and verified or has been witnessed by people I know to be truthful witnesses and I brought much of this evidence with me on my recent tours of America, where there seems to be scant knowledge among Christians of the fast forming Euro superstate. There the evil spirit that came out of

Babylon is again set on world conquest, setting up an empire and image that will be broken only by the return of Jesus in power and great glory.

Chapter 3

The Destruction of Faith and National Pride

Back in January 1989 then-Senator Al Gore introduced the World Environment Policy Act using the line that "the threats we face transcend national boundaries and ideologies." The bill "promotes U.S. participation in international initiatives and global environmental problems such as those initiated under the auspices of the United Nations," according to the *Congressional Record*. Gore went on to produce the overstated environmentalist book *Earth in the Balance* and has even declared the automobile America's public enemy number one! What a narrow escape America had in December 2000—saved by a few hanging chads and lots of prayer! Oddly enough, a globalist environmental line identical to that of Gore's was taken by America's then supposed enemy.

Speaking in December 1988, Michael Gorbachev, then Soviet leader, said: "The world economy is becoming a single organism." He warned against any further extension and intensification of industrialism. Environmentalism, greenism, and false alarms about fantasy "threats" to the planet are all being used to rush along the global agenda, allegedly the only answer to global problems, from supposed climate problems to trade disputes. The world's children are being thoroughly brainwashed to accept this. The British government, for example, in 2001 required primary schools "to incorporate a global dimension into the curriculum." David Blunkett, then Britain's education and employment secretary, told heads that "the content of what is taught must be informed by international and global matters, so preparing pupils to live their lives in a global society."

In maths, for example, children aged five to seven are to "explore number patterns from a range of cultures" while in design and technology they should "develop an empathy for other people's needs." In physical education they are supposed to "perform dances from different cultures," all of it so that they can become "informed, active, responsible global citizens." What we must not do is judge, of course, so an English folk dance must not be presumed in any way superior to a cannibals' jamboree. Of course not . . .

This coming together of cultures and peoples is being urged on nations and established at an astonishing rate. In the *Daily Telegraph*, published in London on August 24, 2000, I saw a report headed: "Fox takes free trade call north of the border." The story soon made clear that the innocent-sounding call for "free trade" was something much more. Vicente Fox, the then newly-elected Mexican president, was calling for a common currency with America and Canada. Said the report, by Philip Delves Broughton: "Since his election last month, Mr. Fox has called on the United States and Canada to help Mexico's development with the aim of creating deeper economic and political ties, similar to the European Union. There is even mention of a common currency." In another report, also in the *Daily Telegraph*, the headline was "New Mexican President urges U.S. to open border."

The article, by Ben Fenton, opened: "Citing the European Union as his model, President Vicente Fox of Mexico has appealed to the United States to open its border to his people and urged closer economic union." The article says that Mr. Fox cited with approval the fact that the EU had helped the poorer European countries, like Greece and Portugal, to catch up with richer countries such as Britain, Germany, and France. He said that he wanted the North American Free Trade Agreement to open the borders between its members—the U.S., Mexico and Canada, "in the same way as the Common Market [the former name of the EU] had been turned into a social and political union." America merging with Mexico? Ridiculous and farfetched? Mr. Fox is already talking about it with George Bush. Politically, of course, this would have the effect of creating a permanent left-wing majority on the North American continent, just as Fabian Socialists rule the new state of Europe, with thirteen of the fifteen member states controlled by left of centre governments at the time of writing.

In October 2000 Mr. Fox arrived in Europe to what the *Financial Times*, Europe's business newspaper, called a red carpet welcome. The paper stated: "Mr. Fox is scheduled to meet kings, presidents and prime ministers in France, Spain, Germany, Belgium and the United Kingdom." It noted that he had already proposed extending the North American Free Trade Agreement into an EU-style common market and said that the plan now was to link Europe more strongly with Mexico.

Mexico's president, Vicente Fox, has toured the world pushing for trade links. These are often the precursor of political links, as in the case of the EU. Watch for all of North and South America to form a single political and economic area. This was from the *Financial Times*.

The same paper said that Caribbean leaders were meeting to consider proposals from Canadian premier Jean Chretien for a free trade area incorporating all the countries of North, Central, and South America and the Caribbean. This would include Cuba. In April 2001, the "Summit of the Americas" in Quebec City, Canada, saw leaders of thirty-four nations sign an accord to create free trade throughout North and South America. The idea is for a creation of a thirty-four–nation free trade area covering eight hundred million people by 2005. Already Washington's relations with Cuba are fast improving, so another impediment to a vast new "common market" has gone. But we know from Europe that what starts as a trading zone soon turns into something much deeper . . .

Open trading borders mean people are also free to move and live where they like. America and Europe are currently being invaded by millions of so-called refugees, most of whom are economic migrants. Some may have more sinister motives. While it is true that a few of them are Christians, most are not, which in Great Britain, home of the Reformation and the country where the Bible was first translated into English, means that there are now millions of residents who owe allegiance to false gods.

Tens of thousands of British-based Moslems marched against Britain in central London during the Gulf War, when this country's armed forces were fighting Saddam. After the terror attacks on America in September 2001 Moslems in Britain and America again shouted slogans against their host countries. This is a wonderful way of weakening a country. In the last war it was termed "the Fifth Column." Another expression which fits is "the enemy within."

With sleeper cells of Islamic terrorists believed to be operating in both our countries, the admission of millions of Islamic peoples whose religion encourages them to act against Christians can be seen to have been, historically, the most dangerous mistake we ever made. Although I recognise that the vast majority of them are economic migrants seeking a better life, they are nevertheless the sea in which the terrorists swim.

Britain, like America, could never be conquered. We both have strong armed forces and are bordered by ocean, wholly so in the case of Britain. But if you allow people to surge into your homeland from all over the world, their allegiance is unlikely to be strong. Therefore opposition to continual watering down of national identity is weakened. In fact, a strong case is being made that national pride is a bad thing, and offensive to those who chose to come and live among us. This influx has also created what the politically correct call a "multi-ethnic society," the perfect excuse to downgrade Christianity's status so that it is now just one of "seven world religions" taught in the classroom. A massive politically correct effort is also being made to degrade our armed forces by allowing women and homosexuals into front-line soldiering. As American and Britain again have to lead the fight for freedom, what shape are our armed forces in? If you were the West's worst enemy and set out to deliberately destroy our military tradition and effectiveness, you couldn't have planned it better.

As I was writing this I heard of a new book by Yoram Hazony, an advisor to the former right-wing Israeli prime minister Binyamin Netanyahu. He writes in *The Jewish State: The Struggle for Israel's*

Soul about how the left in Israel is striking at the roots of state-hood. Everywhere he looks he finds evidence of self-disgust, in uncanny echoes of what has been happening in Britain and, to a lesser extent, in America. Instead of "our country, right or wrong," today's slogan of the universal left is "our country, always wrong." There are even those in America today, the "chattering classes" of the East Coast liberal elite, who blame America for the attacks on New York and Washington. They say, "we had it coming to us." As a reward for feeding the world, perhaps? For even as they denounced the USA or made snide remarks on chat shows, the bulk of the food shipments pouring into Afghanistan had "USA" stamped on them.

Let's put it pithily, as did Rich Lowry in the *National Review:* "Developing mass commercial aviation and soaring skyscrapers was the west's idea; slashing the throats of stewardesses and flying the planes into the skyscrapers was radical Islam's idea." The West, and America in particular, has no need to apologise to the world for much of what it has achieved. When Bin Laden did his "live from the cave" specials on CNN he wore an American-made Timex watch, American ex-army battle fatigues, and talked into infidel-invented mikes and cameras. If he had been left with what his people had invented, he would have been standing in a cave in camel-wool underpants, shouting into the darkness. We do have much to be proud of, unlike him.

In Britain today, pride in Britain's past is almost never taught; instead we get heavy helpings of guilt accompanying our anti–racist lessons. Never was this more clearly seen than when the Dome, Britain's millennium celebration centre, was launched in a blaze of mostly dud fireworks. There were sad little scenes telling us how bad we were to inhabit the earth, as we were making such a mess of it. Weird giant bodies were lit by flashing lights as multicultural mish-mash events swirled around, a cacophony of meaningless-ness which most Britons very wisely avoided. In November 2000 when it was revealed that every visitor to this fiasco had been subsidised to the tune of £100, the only exciting thing that ever happened there occurred: an attempted diamond robbery.

The thieves broke in riding on a JCB digger. They felt they were less conspicuous doing this than coming in through the turnstiles: the whole vast edifice had just sixty-four visitors at the time of the raid! Yet the Dome could have been filled with excitement, scenes showing Great Britain's great triumphs through history, its inventions, like the jet engine, the world's first jet airliner, Concorde, the TV set, the world's first TV service, blacktop roads, railways, steam engines, the tractor, penicillin, the discovery of DNA, splitting the atom, mapping the human genome (jointly with the USA), the world's first industrial revolution, iron smelting, the flush lavatory, radar, the computer, the pocket calculator, the pocket TV, pneumatic tyres and, the most important of all, parliamentary democracy. That, of course, is vanishing very fast in twenty-first century Britain. As I write, the partisan new Labor Speaker of the House of Commons, historically the defender of free speech, has just ordered a Conservative supporter of Israel to leave the chamber. His crime was that he went up to the speaker and—quietly—asked why every speaker called in a debate on the Israeli/Palestinian conflict had been on the side of the Arabs. This MP had clearly failed to understand that in the New World Order Israel *must* be the baddie.

Don't expect democratic fair play or free speech in the New World Order that is taking shape; in Europe there is already talk of banning "extremist" parties, in other words those that do not believe in creating superstates and still believe in patriotism and nation states. These will be called "racist and divisive" and will be banned. Who will decide who the extremists are? Why, the existing majority parties, of course! As for Christian evangelism, that could soon be outlawed! The *Baptist Press* of July 2000 reported that missionaries and lay Christians who share their faith in Jesus could be imprisoned for up to two years under a planned French law that accuses religious proselytisers of "mental manipulation" of the public. French justice minister Elisabeth Guigou reportedly called the bill "a significant advance, giving a democratic state the legal tool to efficiently fight groups abusing its core values."

Repression of true religion will be justified, even in Britain, by examples of how religious cults have brainwashed young people, "kidnapped" teenagers, and so on. The European public will be urged to stick with nice, safe, often state-sponsored religion and to outlaw all these dangerous "cults." This is already happening to some extent, with a media largely ignorant of spiritual matters confusing—deliberately or otherwise—truly dangerous cults with real, non-conformist Christianity. Even the Archbishop of Canterbury, head of the Church of England, gave a long interview in the spring of 2001 praising the spiritual virtues of the New Age movement! Christians have also not been helped by the antics of TV evangelists and spangle-suited so-called "healers" who make fools of themselves and the gospel in equal measure.

In the Christian magazine *Contending Earnestly for the Faith*, it was reported in the April 2000 edition that Brian Houston, president of the Assemblies of God in Australia, appeared on his "Life Is for Living" TV show lying on his back with his feet in the air saying: "We should all be money magnets." Christian congregations all over Britain distinguished themselves in recent years by rolling in the aisles of churches laughing and giggling, while some claimed that gold dust fell on them during services. (I wish!) A friend of mine, who attends one of the more excitable churches in the area, obtained some of this alleged gold dust, took it home, and examined it under a microscope. It seems that it is made of little plastic stars, not unlike fairy dust on sale in Woolworths for young girls to sprinkle in their hair.

Clearly, the god of these churches is economising these days. I am not being irreverent, but I must say that if our Lord wanted to, for example, heal someone's tooth troubles, he would replace their teeth, not fill them with some kind of fool's gold! These are the people we Bible-believing Christians are equated with. The faith has been undermined from within, so do not be surprised if there is little public support for us when the crackdown comes. Incidentally, to those Christians who will rebuke me for finding fault with churches and ministers, I would say that Isaiah, Jeremiah, Ezekiel, and other Old Testament prophets wrote critically of false teachers, as did Paul, John, and Peter in the New Testament, and they named names.

One strong sign that these are the end times is the vast number of false teachers and general apostasy throughout most of the church—just as we were warned would happen before our Lord returns. In Matthew 24:4 Jesus warns us to take heed that no man deceives us, for many shall come in His name saying they are the Christ, deceiving many. The start of the last century saw a major false messiah, Krishnamurti—the so-called great world teacher—appear under the guidance of Theosophists Annie Besant and Charles Leadbeater. But it wasn't the time and he wasn't the right man. The messiah of the New World Order may well shortly appear, for the last days are characterised by religious deception—the greatest such deception the world has ever seen. Never has it been so easy to deceive people as in this Laodicean, untaught church of spiritual ignoramuses.

The EU is the fourth soon-to-be world empire which the Bible clearly tells us will be established before that "great and terrible day." The prophet Daniel foresaw this empire, the revived Roman Empire. He did this in Daniel 2 when he interpreted King Nebuchadnezzar's dream of the empires that would rise and fall upon the earth. This fourth empire, the final world empire, will have ten parts (not necessarily nations) and great "dominion" (Daniel 7:26). It will turn into, not just a world power but *the* world power. "The fourth beast shall be the fourth kingdom upon earth, which shall be diverse from all kingdoms, and shall devour the whole earth, and shall tread it down, and break it in pieces" (Daniel 7:23). The events described in this book clearly show that this empire is almost revived and will shortly strut on to the world stage, with its own charismatic leader, full of bombast and performing "lying wonders." This is the man who will make the peace treaty with Israel and break it after three and a half years, halfway through the Great Tribulation (Daniel 9:27).

Otmar Issing, a member of the German Central Bank Council, the Bundesbank, said when the euro was being created: "There is no example in history of a lasting monetary union that was not linked to political union." When the Common Market was being talked about in Britain, we were all assured that it was "just about trade." Trade, we were all agreed, was a good thing. Britain, the first country to industrialise, has been a world trader for hundreds of years, so obviously we, the British people, were all for more trade. What could be more innocent? Yet nobody was ever asked if they wished to become a citizen of the EU, which is what our passports now say we are. In the infamous Maastricht Treaty under Article 8, "Citizenship of the Union," it states:

1. Citizenship of the Union is hereby established. Every person holding the nationality of a member state shall be a citizen of the Union.
2. Citizens of the Union shall enjoy the rights conferred by this treaty and shall be subject to the duties imposed thereby.

British Prime Minister Blair's "superpower" vision of Europe is backed by EU head Romano Prodi.

Romano Prodi, the former Italian prime minister so beloved of his people that they nicknamed him "the greasy sausage," is in no doubt where Europe and the world are heading. This man, who heads the European Commission, making him the nearest thing Europe has to an American president, published a paper called "Strategic Objectives 2000-2005: Shaping the New Europe." In it he says:

Over the next decade we will complete our integration and give shape to a new political Europe. The next five years will be decisive. We are already pushing forward with political integration. Political integration will become a reality. What we are aiming at, therefore, is a new kind of global governance to manage the global economy and environment. . . .

The Commission intends to propose the creation of a truly integrated European transport area, through the creation of a single airspace. So there'll be a blue (European) flag flying over the white cliffs of Dover, symbol of Britain's resistance to "European integration" in the last war, when the heroes of the Royal Air Force refused to surrender the integrity of our air space. They needn't have bothered, as there are plans for Britain, France, and Germany to share embassies—a clear prelude to them becoming one nation, with the rest of the ill-assorted Euro ensemble.

Europe will become more closely integrated and at the same time the Union will embark on a process of enlargement leading ultimately to the unification of our continent, says Mr. Prodi. In a rare flash of insight though, Prodi gave the quote of the millennium—so far. Asked by the newspaper *Sueddeutsche Zeitung* what he regarded as the biggest mistake made by Brussels so far, he replied: "Me." Well, he said it . . .

Few people have so far heard the first distant trumpet calls to the next and final step in creating a one-world economic and then political zone. To discern these you have to read the business pages of serious newspapers. Already there has been the odd article in the *Financial Times* postulating the idea of one currency for the world. However, a heavyweight player showed his hand in September 2000. Robert Mundell, the Nobel prize-winning economist credited with dreaming up the euro, held a seminar with Hans Tietmeyer, former president of the Bundesbank, the German central bank. Mr. Mundell, a Canadian academic, was quoted in the *Daily Telegraph* as saying he was not content with a single European currency and suggested there should be a global one as well. "It would be much easier to achieve—at least from a technical point of view—than people think," he was quoted as saying. "We need to move towards a system that would stabilise not just the world price level, but also exchange rates among major currency areas."

Linking the finances of Europe's countries is just stage one. Just as in Israel Labor politician Shimon Peres says national political organisations are old hat, and "welfare and freedom can only be ensured within a wider framework, on a regional or even super-regional basis," so in Europe and around the world Socialist leaders are blurring national sovereignty. The nation state is recognised across the globe as the universal enemy of the New World Order. It will soon disappear. How good it is when driving through America to see masses of Old Glories flying on flagpoles. How wonderful to be proud of one's country. In Britain flag flying has been largely stamped out; councils simply refuse planning permission for flagpoles.

Gerald Howarth, MP for Aldershot and a great patriot, sticks a Union Jack over the stars of Europe on his car plate.

Gerald Howarth, a friend of mine, a member of Parliament for Aldershot, and a doughty fighter against the Eurostate, was pictured in a front-page newspaper story written by my wife on May 3, 2001. He was shown committing what was soon to become a criminal act in Britain—putting a small Union Jack on his car's number plate. Since September 2001, motorists who display the Union flag on their number plates can be stopped by police and prosecuted. The headline I wrote on this story was: "It's a crime to be patriotic." Only the European flag, with its twelve gold stars of the Madonna, will be allowed on the registration plates of new cars in the future. The law was passed by the huge Socialist majority in Britain's parliament in April 2001. Said Gerald Howarth:

I see this as another attempt to foist a European identity on this country.

We have a European Parliament, a European Court, a European currency, a European anthem and a European flag, and we are about to have a European army. So we have all those symbols of nation statehood. Our driving licences have to have the Euro symbol—we cannot have the Union flag—and now our registration plates will have it as well. It is an affront to the British people to authorise motorists to bear the Euro symbol on their cars and make it a criminal offence for Englishmen to proudly proclaim the cross of St. George.

Britain's new picture driving licenses, complete with EU logo, which could double up as identity cards.

In an article in the paper I edited, Gerald continued: "It is no good people telling us we're being paranoid about this. Every new measure is designed to drive us into this country called Europe. Why else couldn't we have our very distinctive flag? Everybody knows what the Union Jack is, but no, that's not good enough." Pointing out that the new law from Europe also banned individualised number plates, the MP concluded: "The new law is also a spoilsport measure which crushes individuality and choice."*

Where flags fly, the Euro flag (Madonna's stars) is given the same status as national flags. Europhiles will no longer have to seek permission to fly the Euro flag; in future, according to proposals put forward in 2000 by deputy prime minister John Prescott, the EU banner will be treated as the symbol of a nation state. MEP Nigel Farage said: "This gives the EU flag the same formal recognition as a national flag. . . . Labor is finally admitting that we are just one part of a giant European superstate. Labor has always maintained the EU was just about free trade. Now it recognises that we [Britain] are a mere part of the superstate. This should be treated as an admission of honesty at last."

I had an interesting letter from a patriotic Roman Catholic man early in 2001. He was complaining that the Euro flag was flying without authority all through Britain and that this was an insult to his Madonna. This is further confirmation that the stars have a religious symbolism, but clearly most lay Catholics haven't a clue what this really signals—the aim of a united Catholic Europe dedicated to "our lady." However, a strict warning from the EU bosses—the commissioners—bans anti-European groups from using the stars logo. Apparently the commission fears they might write something rude across it . . .

A group of so-called "wise men" set out plans to shake up the EU in a document delivered at the dawn of the new millennium. The theme was allowing a membership of "25 to 30 or even more

---

* Following furious protests from patriots, the British government announced on December 28, 2001, that British motorists wanting to display the Union Jack on their number plates instead of the Euro symbol wil now be able to do so without being fined. A small victory for freedom!

Ecuador to push ahead on plan for dollarisation

Australia 'open minded' on NZ currency union

Argentina studies dollar plan

Why stop at the euro?

Feature stories about the worldwide push for monetary union, ultimately leading to a one-world currency called, perhaps, the Earth Dollar. The euro's full title is already the "eurodollar"—watch soon for the AsiaDollar. The currency of Hong Kong is already linked to the U.S. dollar.

participants." They criticised "sluggish decision making" and called for a strengthening of the authority of the president—echoes of that "strong man" again. It said that the use of national vetoes throttled EU decision making and promoted more decisions by majority vote. The days of the nation state are fast drawing to a close in Europe, and not just Europe, as we see phase one of the plan for world government being rapidly implemented, as Revelation 13 describes.

In May 2000 Robert Mundell was in South America—again urging the merging of currencies. Nobel prizewinner Mundell was on a lecture tour of Brazil expounding the virtues of a single currency for Mercosur, the South American trade group that also includes Argentina, Uruguay and Paraguay. According to Britain's *Financial Times*, Europe's leading business newspaper, as a first step in a process of economic convergence, "advised the region's countries to link their currencies to the U.S. dollar." He said that interest rates would then soon fall to the U.S. level.

Many countries already use the dollar as a substitute currency for their own debased notes; Russia is one example. El Salvador became the latest country to trade in its currency for the dollar, on January 1, 2001. This telling quote comes from the *Financial Times* of December 29, 2000: "El Salvador, bursting with 6.5 million people and possessing few natural resources, has decided swimming with the global tide is the only way to survive." In May 2001, Guatemala became the latest Latin American country to succumb to the dollar when employees were allowed to ask for their pay in the U.S. currency. Latin America's drift to the dollar started when Equador adopted it in 2000. The signing of the plan for a free trade area throughout the Americas by 2005 will hasten the trend. The global tide sweeps all before it. Incidentally, the full title of the euro is the eurodollar—so when all currencies are merged even the name change will hardly be noticed.

Mr. Mundell beavered over to Asia in February 2001, and I spotted this headline in the *Financial Times* on February 9: "Call for Asian monetary union." The article began: "Robert Mundell, the Nobel Prize-winning economist, has reignited the debate about the dangers of currency instability by calling for the creation of an Asian monetary union. Mr. Mundell said that exchange rate volatility between the Japanese yen and the U.S. dollar was a problem for Asian countries. The creation of a common currency area, on the pattern of the euro-zone, would be highly desirable." It is also becoming more of a possibility. Here is a quote from Jorge Braga de Macedo, president of the OECD Development Centre: "Just a year ago an Asian currency was unthinkable. But increasing signs that Asian states are devising a currency protection system and looking more closely at each other's policies makes it at least something worth talking about."

This fascinating full-page advertisement, also from the *FT*, Europe's leading business newspaper, was placed by a Swiss bank when the Euro was launched. It clearly shows the plan for the future world currency. The Y is the yen, the E is the euro, and the S is the dollar.

That the next step is already mapped out is something I found by accident while reading the financial news. There, again in the *Financial Times*, read by bankers and heads of industry, was a full page advertisement from a Swiss bank. It just had one word on it in giant type. It read: "Yes." The y was the yen, the e was the euro and the s was the dollar. Another thing I noticed on a flight to America, as I read the business pages, was how close the values of the three main currencies are. They could all be nudged to parity very easily and, hey, presto, we have the single currency for the coming one-world government.

Those around the world who like to keep their assets in cash, stuffed in the mattress away from the taxman's prying eyes, had better beware. As the world switches to its new currency, hoarders will have a problem. Many Europeans discovered this as the time approached for them to turn in their national currencies in favor of the euro, the one currency for all Europe. The date chosen for the euro to become legal tender was January 2002 and citizens of the superstate were allowed six months to convert their existing money into euros. This posed a problem in places like France and Italy, where the tradition of working for cash is strong. Hard though it is to believe, not all of this cash had been declared to the authorities. Rich misers were in trouble.

The Bank of France, for example, calculated that £15 billion in banknotes was tucked away in French peasants' little nest eggs. If they brought this money out in the open, to change it into the new currency, they risked having to explain how they acquired it in the first place. Money laundering regulations already meant that deposits of over £5,000 had to be reported to the revenue. It seems banks began getting lots of calls from bewildered of Boulogne . . . wanting to know what would become of his money. While some started changing their money a little bit at a time, to avoid attracting attention, others decided to take the old route to hiding earnings, by buying jewellery, antiques, and anything else that could be tucked away. Globalisation has a price, even for those who happily voted for a united Europe.

With the increasing globalisation of companies and giant takeovers happening frequently, it is clear that the leading companies operate outside the control of any one government. Readers of business newspapers, like the *Financial Times*, see non-stop references to globalism, global thinking, global action, global alliances and global affairs. "Business urged to help promote global change" was a typical headline in October 2000. "Business today is permanently under a global spotlight," United Nations' development program director Mark Malloch Brown told a business audi-

The cover of a British magazine for company directors. It highlights the trend to globalization.

ence in London. What could be more natural, then, than a world government to supervise all this global business? Global warming (or not), global pollution, global problems—everything seems to be crying out for global solutions.

In September 2000 the United Nations in New York was the scene of a global government conference designed to examine the future of tne world, no less. The aim was to: "Create an organisational structure whereby the peoples of the world can participate effectively in global decision-making in the context of the United Nations system." In preparation for this unprecedented conference, "Charter 99: A Charter for Global Democracy" called for all nations to adopt principles of "international accountability, justice and sustainable development."

Called "The Millennium Assembly and Summit," the meeting was part of the UN's latest initiative to bring in global government. In 1942 this was clearly foreseen by British science fiction writer H. G. Wells, a Fabian Socialist and one-world government advocate, who predicted: "There will be no day of days . . . when a new world order comes into being. Step-by-step and here and there it will arrive." Leftist thinkers like Wells and playwright George Bernard Shaw helped pave the intellectual way for this satanic institution, fulfilling the dream of Lenin, who wrote in *State and Revolution:* "We set ourselves the ultimate aim of destroying the state."

Paving the way for the UN's meeting, Charter 99 was sponsored by a consortium of influential nongovernmental organisations —the lobbyists. Among them were groups like the One World Trust, the Royal Commonwealth Society, and the World Federalist Association. This last organisation is well advanced on its blueprint for a one-world government, publishing masses of documents detailing "the Constitution for the Federation of Earth," the world judiciary (an idea already far advanced), the world executive, the world parliament, etc. I have copies of all these documents, having inquired of the organisation and being rewarded with an invitation to attend their annual delegate meeting.

The location rather put me off—it was in Baghdad, courtesy of Saddam Hussein. Saddam, by the way, is rebuilding Babylon, using bricks with his name on one side and King Nebuchadnezzar on the other. Why be modest when you are rebuilding one of the wonders of the ancient world? To see the prophesied fate of the rebuilt Babylon, turn to Revelation 18. The first attempt at establishing a new world order was at the Tower of Babel, established by Nimrod, whose name is taken from a Hebrew word which means "rebel." Those trying to rebuild Babel today, the heart of a godless one-world system, to be headed by Antichrist, the ultimate rebel, have learned nothing from history and will assuredly face God's judgement if they do not repent.

Chapter 4

A Church Service for Wizards

The world is in a mess because the church is in a mess giving, in most cases, no Bible-based moral leadership. As Western society ceases to base its values on core Christianity, it gets crueller and more uncaring. The elderly are neglected and over thirty-eight percent of all births in Britain are to single mothers. Euthanasia takes root in Holland and looks set to spread as the talk is of "scarce resources" and "too many people," which encourages mass abortion resulting, in the USA alone, in the murder of forty-three million babies.

Meanwhile the homosexual agenda advances everywhere, with countries advertising "pink" destinations, like Newcastle, England. Endless new laws on equality mean churches may have to marry homosexuals in South Africa, while Vermont has passed a law allowing this very thing, sparking a backlash campaign with the slogan: "Take back Vermont." The homosexual "velvet mafia" in Hollywood turns out anti-family films which deride ordinary relationships.

The armed forces of the West have to tolerate "gays" while many women of the twenty-first century try to prove they are the equal of men in drinking and bad behaviour.

Meanwhile, anything goes on British TV, with transvestite contests and nude game shows. The only clampdown is on anyone allegedly hurting "Mother Earth"—the old witchcraft concept of the earth goddess. A dog owner who allowed his pet to walk out of a country park in Britain with a stick in its mouth was traced and prosecuted, taken to court, and fined. You can blaspheme, murder babies, turn truth on its head, and deny the Ten Commandments, but boy, you'd better not offend old "Mother" or you are in serious trouble.

The Archbishop of York, number two man in the Church of England hierarchy, commissioned a new catechism which was published in June 2001. It declares that homosexuality is divinely ordered. The catechism was described in the press as a radical rethink of church teaching on homosexuality. Written by Canon Edward Norman, canon and treasurer of the great cathedral of York Minster, it seeks to define a new, "inclusive" Anglicanism for the first time since Thomas Cranmer wrote *The Book of Common Prayer* in 1662.The new catechism says that "homosexuality may not be a condition to be regretted but to have divinely ordered and positive qualities." Archbishop of York Dr. David Hope wants the catechism as a tool for use in training ministers. Dr. Hope has described his own sexuality as "a grey area" and says he is celibate.

Harry Potter has been used as a theme in a Church of England service, with the vicar dressed as a wizard.

Because most of the church long since ceased to believe in biblical fundamentals, all kinds of weirdness crops up in churches. Take the Harry Potter books which, popular as they are, are based solely around an academy for witches and concentrate on spells and sorcery at a place known as Hogwarts. As such you would imagine no pastor or priest would touch the books with a wizard's wand. But you would be wrong. A church in my hometown of Guildford, Surrey, England, has been attempting to lure in the young using a Harry Potter theme. The vicar in the Church of England (Episcopal) church held a family service featuring wizards, pointy hats, broomsticks, and a game of quidditch, taken from the books.

A member of the Church of England pretends to consult a crystal ball at a church fundraiser.

The Hogwarts liturgy, posted on an internet site, was, according to the

Times of London, welcomed by other clergy who wished to adopt it for their churches as well. Evangelical Christians, however, denounced the scheme as "importing evil symbols into the church." As if to prove them right, a banner showing a serpent, representing the House of Slytherin in the bestselling books by J. K. Rowling, was stretched across the church of All Saints at Guildford. Banners of the three other Hogwarts houses (each boy at the mythical school belongs to a "house") were also displayed.

The church door was transformed, as if by a spell, into the gateway to "Platform 9 and three-quarters," a magical platform supposedly sited at London's Kings Cross Station. This is where, in Rowling's books, children catch the Hogwarts express to Hogwarts School of Wizardry. The Rev. Brian Coleman, vicar of All Saints, wore wizards' clothes for the event, complete with magical hat and cloak, as he played the role of Albus Dumbledore, the headmaster of Hogwarts, in leading the service. Michael Truman, a member of the parish about to qualify as a lay reader, a position in the Church of England which would allow him to take part in services and rituals, played a part in the whole sorry affair. He has written a "Harry Potter liturgy" as a variation on an authorised Church of England service, in the church's new "Common Worship" service book. He played a teacher in the church production, while his eleven-year-old son Mark played Harry Potter. The service featured "muggle songs" as hymns, while the whole charade ended with a game of quidditch in which "worshippers" competed to capture a "snitch"—a yellow rubber ball.

All Saints Church chose a Sunday in September because the New Testament reading in the C of E liturgical calendar, James 1:17–27, was considered particularly appropriate to the themes of Harry Potter. As the *Times* explained: "A broomstick, an 'invisibility cloak' and 'ton-tongue toffees' will be used to illustrate verse 17, about generous gifts coming from God. Mr. Coleman conceded that the service might not receive universal approbation. 'But if you look at *The Narnia Chronicles* by C. S. Lewis, these are books that also use magic as the background to a story.'" Mr. Coleman went on to use the old argument that the Harry Potter books are "highly moral" and are about loyalty, standing up for friends and supporting good over evil. "This is exactly what the passage in James is all about," said Mr. Coleman. "Young folk are all very much into Harry Potter. We are using this interest."

However, evil cannot be used to fight evil, and the Bible makes clear that witchcraft is one of the things God hates most, so any symbolism involving witchcraft is completely out of place in church, to put it mildly. Fortunately Britain's Evangelical Alliance, an umbrella group of the more Bible-believing elements of British Christianity, did point out that while clergy should certainly connect with contemporary culture, using symbols associated with evil would confuse children.

In some Anglican (Episcopalian) parishes in England there are even events described as "Christian seances." David Christie-Murray, a former schoolmaster at Harrow, one of Britain's top schools, was reported in the *Sunday Times* (London) of August 8, 2000, to be urging parishes in the Church of England to encourage worshippers to develop their "psychic skills." He said he wants churches to set up a "Christian rescue group," or séance, to help the souls of atheists and others who have "passed over to the other side." He believes such souls to be "lost and bewildered, in a condition in which they did not believe in this life and cannot understand now that they have passed over into the next." He says there is evidence that the dead can communicate with the living.

When I was a young man inquiring into spiritual things, I too was drawn to the occult. Two neighbours who were spiritists aroused my interest in communicating with "the other side" and I was soon a regular attendee at spiritualist services. They read carefully selected bits from the Bible, giving a vague cloak of respectability to the whole farce, but oddly, I never heard the following passage read out which lays down God's laws:

> There shall not be found among you any one that maketh his son
> or his daughter to pass through the fire, or that useth divination,
> or an observer of times, or an enchanter, or a witch, or a charmer,
> or a consulter with familiar spirits, or a wizard, or a necroman-

cer. For all that do these things are an abomination unto the Lord: and because of these abominations the Lord thy God doth drive them out from before thee. Thou shalt be perfect with the Lord thy God."

—Deuteronomy 18:10–13

God goes on to make it clear that those nations who follow diviners and occultists will be brought down. The West is currently riddled with "psychics" and "psychic fairs" like a cancer, eating into the body of society. Most weeks the newspaper I edit carries advertisements for several major psychic events in our circulation area, comprising over two hundred thousand readers. These commercial organisations book the largest halls in the various towns, filling them with "Britain's top international psychics, mediums, clairvoyants, palmists, tarot consultants. . . ." This typical advertisement, selected at random from the first edition I picked up, goes on: "Their accuracy will shock you (readings extra), also aura photography. Plus a fantastic selection of mystic craft and crystal stalls selling tarot cards, crystals, jewellery, oils, music, Indian artefacts and much more."

Admission is £2.50, children free. There are a great many of these travelling psychic road shows going round fleecing the public, rather like the dubious medicine men of the old American West. A friend went to see a gipsy fortune teller, paying £5. After spouting a rambling load of nonsense, she turned to him and said: "Now the gipsy will grant you any wish you want." He said: "I wish I could have my £5 back." She threw him out instead . . .

I could save all these sad customers their admission money, for I have been through all that and came out the other side, grateful to be breathing cleaner air. I lost count of the number of times "mediums" placed me up against a wall to inspect my "aura," then asked me to repeat the exercise. I never saw a thing, but they persisted, as they had the delusion that I was going to amount to something in the world of psychics. If only they could have seen the future . . .

There was one occasion in which the demon spirit controlling a medium did give a flash of insight about the future, in truly odd circumstances. My wife Patricia and I, ever ready to seek psychic thrills in those days, were calling at the house of an old friend, a man with advanced skills in contacting "spirits." Our purpose was to sit in a so-called development circle in which our psychic powers would be developed. These sessions were a hoot, as a small group of us sat around in a darkened room, listening to scratchy old Johnny Cash tapes. It seems the spirits liked country and western music. (They obviously didn't know Johnny Cash was a Christian.) Anyway, on this particular evening we arrived at their home, the door opened, and there was a lady I will call Agatha, our host's wife and herself an experienced medium. "Ah," she said, "it's Alan and Pat. One day you are going to expose us." With that she smiled and led us into the house.

It was an odd experience, but the voice had the ring of truth. I am sure "Agatha" had no idea what she had just blurted out. She was used to her body being taken over by what she thought were spirits of the dead but which were in fact demons, sent to earth to create confusion and evil among gullible and vulnerable people.

Indeed her pronouncement was true. We do our best to expose spiritualism for what it really is—contact with demons masquerading as dead people. "Agatha's" spirit guide was correct (and this is the only instance we know of when it was right).

Madame Blavatsky, founder of the Theosophical Society and mother of the New Age movement, similarly got her odd ideas from telepathic communications from alleged "masters." These "masters," like Agatha's, were actually demons. Today there is a vogue for contacting "angels," with TV shows devoted to people retelling their supernatural experiences. I believe that on at least two occasions God has sent an angel to save my life. However, we are not to try and seek out angels, for this is unbiblical. The only angels contacted in this way will be fallen ones—otherwise known as demons.

I can tell you that "the friends," as Agatha and her husband called the spirits, never did them much good. Their lives staggered from one disaster to another, one catastrophe to the next. They never made a move in business without holding a séance and getting top-level advice from the spirit world. As a result they moved houses, started businesses, and created havoc wherever they went, leaving a trail of misery, confusion, and unpaid debts. Tomorrow was always going to be triumphant, but unfortunately it never was. Because I was an impressionable young man looking for a father figure, I went to work full time for this couple's ragbag organisation, seeing at firsthand the double dealing, duplicity, and downright lies that characterised the "New Age movement."

The fact that modern "seers" and psychics constantly get things wrong doesn't seem to harm their careers. Not one foretold the September 2001 attacks on America, for instance. Yet if you look in any major newsagents, you will see stacks of unpleasant looking magazines, often featuring crystal balls on their covers. They are full of tips on things that don't matter very much and a high proportion of them carry New Year predictions every January. All of them are made by people with no track record of success, to put it mildly, yet millions of gullible people turn to them.

I once worked for a newspaper where one of my jobs was to make sure the horoscope column fitted in its space on the page. We would blithely swap the star signs around to make them fit the space, so Taurus might go in under Pisces, etc. I have no doubt people believed them, as I often notice that the star signs are the first thing people turn to in their newspaper. "Let's see what our luck is today." This is the sort of asinine, meaningless waffle you get from deluded people at psychic fairs. I just wonder how many other sub-editors and editors swap the star signs around to make them fit an awkward space in the page!

Madame Blavatsky received her satanic, "telepathic" delusions until her death in 1891. She wrote: "The Christians and scientists must be made to respect their Indian betters. The wisdom of India, her philosophy and achievement, must be made known in Europe and America and the English be made to respect the natives of India and Tibet more than they do" (from *The Golden Book of the Theosophical Movement*, 1925.) How this philosophy has swept the West, with Indian gurus leading pop stars by the nose, Indian religion influencing much of Western thought, and yoga classes in many church halls. Yet anyone with common sense could take one look at India and see that, in its spiritual life at least, it has nothing to teach us.

Because of Hinduism, millions of mangy cows are worshipped and allowed to wander at will, causing traffic accidents. Billions of rats munch their way through the country's corn stores, secure in the knowledge the Indians dare not kill them, lest they be reincarnated as rats. The caste system ensures that millions are born to debt and spend their lives in slavery. There is still widespread discrimination against the up to two hundred million Untouchables, now known as Dalits, or those outside the Hindu-based caste system around which everything in Indian society revolves. Especially in rural areas, these modern Untouchables can find only the very worst jobs to do, like scavenging, clearing excrement, and disposing of dead animals. Even after the Gujarat earthquake of early 2001 there were complaints about lower caste people being denied aid and relief workers said that different castes refused to live together in tented shelters.

The whole of India is a mess from top to bottom, unable to adequately feed and clothe its people or look after its sick, despite an intelligent population, rich soil, and as many natural advantages as, say, America or Britain. The reasons are obvious even in news film from the country, the latest of which showed a five-legged cow which turned up at a Ganges festival and was declared "holy." All of its by-products then commanded high prices, with some people daft enough to pay to drink its urine. Tens of millions—as many as seventy million—turned up for this festival of Kumbh Mela, which was uncritically reported nightly in Britain on Channel Four, which will not allow real Christians to appear to defend their faith.

Tony Pearce, in his *Light for the Last Days* newsletter, commented:

> As the Kumbh Mela was coming to an end, the state of Gujarat was shaken by an earthquake, the worst to hit India since 1950. A thousand miles to the east the worshippers at the Kumbh Mela felt the ground sway under them. I do not wish to say that the

catastrophe which fell on the poor people of Gujarat was a judgement because of what their fellow Hindus were doing on the banks
of the Ganges. But the shaking ground is a graphic picture of the
reality that this kind of religious activity is "a house on the sand"
which cannot give security with God to those who engage in it."

If you wish to see the fruits of New Age/Hindu thought, take a trip
to India. But take plenty of water purifiers and get some good medical insurance.

The idea of the New Agers I worked for was that we were to
help usher in the age of Aquarius, just like in the song. We would
publish newspapers, which would ostensibly look like any other
newspapers. However, they would have a hidden spiritual agenda.
This is basically that man is god and man created God in his own
image, a blasphemous reversal of the truth, but standard New Age
thought. These people knew a garbled version of the Book of Revelation, so understood that the world as we know it was about to
end, with earthquakes, giant hailstones, fire, and famine and everything else the Bible describes.

When these terrible times came upon the world, we thought
we would be ready to offer spiritual guidance, as our leader was an
advanced holy man—in his own estimation anyway. He talked of
attending psychic summits while hovering over Tibet, where the
great ones apparently lurk, waiting for their big moment. These
are the "masters," spiritual beings or chosen men who have evolved
to a higher level than the rest of us. New Agers would say these
masters include Buddha, Mohammed, Confucius, and even Jesus!

Jesus gave the lie to this by telling people that the Father was
the source of His authority. Yet every guru, for example, says his
authority came from his guru, down a long line of gurus. Jesus is
unique, "the only begotten Son of God," as the Bible puts it. However, when the Antichrist arrives, they will say he is the latest man
to be inhabited by the "christ consciousnesss," which ties in with
their belief that "all world religions have common truths which
transcend potential differences." The coming one-world religion
has Hindu/Buddhist roots and they are happy for you to worship

pagan deities from Pan to Brahma, Vishnu and Shiva to Lucifer himself. On the other hand, I believe there are sinister plans for those who are monotheistic—Christians, Jews, and Muslims. Beware. William Penn, the God-fearing Englishman who founded Pennsylvania, warned: "If men will not be governed by God, then they must be governed by tyrants."

Because the alternative health movement, the nuts and nutcases fraternity, is also very interested in things "spiritual," as long as they exclude our Lord Jesus Christ, it was decided that our New Age offshoot should launch a health magazine. Unfortunately, our leader had no concept of copyright or much else in the way of the law, so "borrowed" a large number of advertisements from an existing health magazine. He ended up in legal trouble and the whole project was quickly dropped. Another of those little problems the "friends" from the other side had inconveniently missed.

For those who would place their faith in mediums, New Agers, crystals, astologers, and spiritual mumbo-jumbo, take a lesson from someone who went through all that thirty years ago, long before it became fashionable, and found out the hard way that it was a load of complete rubbish. Under the guidance of people who regarded themselves as the top mediums in the country, we crashed into crisis after crisis. We even managed to almost bankrupt a millionairess who was a follower of "our leader," who had a taste for attractive women especially when they were loaded. Incidentally, the leader never used old fashioned words like "spiritualist." Hitler, probably the biggest one-man disaster of the twentieth century, consulted astologers before every major move. Today's specialists in psychic dud advice are "channellers" and New Agers. It's the same old story, the same old lies. As our friend Jacob Prasch says, when people say God is doing a new thing, what is actually happening is that Satan is doing a very old thing.

Satan has no new tricks, but then people are so gullible and ill-informed that the old ones repeatedly suffice, and never more so than in these end times, when Satan, knowing that his time is short, goes round like a roaring lion, seeking whom he may devour. In the New Age organisation I worked for, there was great delight if a

"star name" could be brought on board. They would be used ruth-
lessly and wrung out to the last charity performance and bundle of
cash. One such man, still a top TV performer and showbiz personality, got involved after his son was brought in for "healing." Healing, by the way, is another great money-spinning scam, used exten-
sively by fraudsters of all kinds, from allegedly Christian money-
preachers and TV exhibitionists to myriads of "alternative" practitioners.

"I declare you heeeeeled" they bellow, but the poor victims go
home in their wheelchairs. My wife once interviewed a psychic
healer who went into a trance and was "taken over" by an alleged
Chinese doctor who spoke with a man's voice. This is classic demonic possession and often happens in spiritist circles. However,
what were the fruits? Not only were no people healed, but one
terrible night this woman's close relatives were killed in a car crash
after leaving her house—something her "powers" had failed to predict.

For over a year I watched sick people brought into the New
Age "surgery" where I worked. I never saw anyone healed. What I
did see was a dependency formed, so that the sick person would
develop a great if unwarranted faith in the healer, who was expert
at soothing talk and false promises. The sick person would then
start coming regularly, not forgetting to leave a bundle of cash in
the offerings basket. The "treatment" consisted of the laying on of
hands backed up with pseudo-medical gibberish and the implica-
tion that the healer had vast medical knowledge and training. This
was untrue; to the best of my knowledge he had been on nothing
more than a naval first aid course, if that. To add to the spiritual
ambience, he had a life-size image of the Shroud of Turin on the
wall of his "surgery." Two fakes for the price of one!

If you ever questioned any of this, it would be explained that
his qualifications were gained in previous lives, under great masters of the day. There is no answer to that, of course, except to say
the Bible clearly teaches that it is given man to live once and then
to die. There are no second circuits, no chances to come back to
put things right in endless cycles of "doing a little better each time,"

as the Buddhists teach. We will never reach perfection on earth. Our righteousness is, as Paul put it, as filthy rags. Our only means of having our sins washed away is by the blood of Jesus. No so-called healer can heal you. Because sickness and disease come from Satan, he can take away that which he has put on people. However, I often noticed that people "healed" of a minor ailment later developed a more serious or fatal one. Many New Agers do have psychic powers and can perform certain lying signs and wonders, but no long term good comes of any of it, especially for the practitioners.

The TV star's son was never healed, nor was there the possibility that he could have been. But the man was hooked for a while and raised a lot of cash for the "cause," although what exactly the cause was often eluded me, as our organisation lurched first one way and then another. One day I arrived at our leader's house to find his extensive back garden being dug up by bulldozers, as he tried to create a mini golf course in his yard. Like everything else he attempted, it was never planned or properly executed. The last day I saw the place, it was a lunar landscape of huge mounds and stagnant pools of water. The leader had become bored and moved on to the next ridiculous project.

Remember, the point I am making is that these are the people who would dare to offer you their advice on living. These are the people with familiar spirits the Bible warns about, this is the real world of the cute little apprentice wizards of that nice lady J. K. Rowling, the author that naïve vicars think is "right on." As they seek to find truth in Hindu writings, contact "ETs," the latest name for demons, or chant "Om," repeatedly, this sorry crew get more and more confused. For Satan is the father of lies and the author of confusion. If there is a philosophy you cannot understand, it is almost certainly satanic and designed to ensure you waste your life following riddles and will o' the wisps. Freemasonry is a good example of this.

You never saw a more sorry, sick, crisis-ridden group of people than those I met in psychic circles. Ill-health was a common condition, as they reaped the fruits of disobeying God. Divorce, bankruptcy, and all-round bad judgment—these were their specialities. Advice? Certainly, if you wanted to know what not to do in any situation. I was billeted with a way-out lady who thought she was in touch with Venusians. As with most of the crowd, she was a vegetarian, as all the gurus are. Like Hindus, they believed that this would help you get more in touch with your spiritual self and the great cosmic universe. I have nothing against vegetarianism, although our Lord said that everything is sanctified for us to eat. However, I have noticed that sometimes vegetarianism goes hand in hand with way out spiritual nuttiness and muddled, New Age ideas.

Our great New Age leader and his wife were allegedly vegetarian, just like Adolf Hitler, on the grounds that this helped the cosmic consciousness flow through them, whatever that was supposed to mean. However, their belief systems were flexible, as I found out when I stumbled into the leader's office one day to find him munching a meat pie. "What are you doing?" I asked, deeply shocked, for in those early days I thought they really did practise what they preached. The leader looked at me with some irritation and snapped "Needs must, old son—I haven't got time to bother with all that vegetarian -------." This was when I started the process of finding out that psychics, New Agers, crystal ball gazers—the whole grisly crew—have very flexible principles. "Needs must, old son," I was told on repeated occasions when incredible lies were told about our newspaper's circulation, for example. "Our need is greater than theirs and they can afford it," was another justification given to me. Our cause was important, so cheating, stealing—almost anything—could be justified. There was even boasting that when one man had started campaigning against the healing ministry, they had all gathered round to pray for him to die—and he allegedly had.

I discovered that money given to the "cause" was sometimes grabbed in handfuls from the collection basket to be used by "Agatha" for playing bingo. I learned that money given for the purposes of healing was diverted to prop up ailing business enterprises. I found that stupendous lies could be told in furtherance of the cause, which in those days I believed to be Christian. After all, didn't they have that huge picture of the Shroud on the wall of the healing sanctuary? Pat and I later discovered this is a sure sign of a cult or "ism," by the way—these objects are there to create an illusion of holiness to fool those who do not know the Bible. In fact the Bible teaches that we (and our churches) should have no images or statues which people can venerate. "Thou shalt not make thee any graven image, or any likeness of anything that is in heaven above, or that is in the earth beneath, or that is in the waters beneath the earth: thou shalt not bow down thyself unto them, nor serve them . . ." (Deuteronomy 5:8–9).

Chapter 5

Deadly Deceptions

If you are attending a church which meets in a building featuring statues and religious objects, leave at once. You are in the wrong church. This is man's idea of "religion," not God's and its evil roots are in the pagan worship of ancient Babylon, where there were popular religious images of the mother and child, images that crop up in pagan religions scattered throughout the world. They were literally scattered, by God, when he confused the language at Babel. Now, both religious and political Babylon are being rebuilt, primarily in Europe but also in America and elsewhere. The "great whore church" of Revelation is being created before our eyes and it crops up in unexpected situations and places. Alongside it is the New Age movement, which also has its roots in Babylonian mysticism.

I have always wanted to own and run newspapers, filling them with content of my own choosing. After all, even editors only have limited freedom to print what they want: go too far in a direction your owners disapprove of and you quickly become an ex-editor. So a few years ago Pat and I were intrigued to see a new Christian newspaper being published out of Independence, Missouri—which happens to be Pat's home state. A friend of ours, an ordained minister, began writing articles for this publication which, on the face of it, was a well produced broadsheet paper using a lot of color.

Pat and I arranged to go and meet the publishers in their Independence headquarters. When we first arrived a few distant warning bells began to ring, as the stairs down to their basement offices were lined with paintings of the apostles. Odd, we thought. Nobody knows what the apostles looked like . . .

Down in the basement, where the people who edited and directed the paper were working, were large paintings of Christ on the walls. This we thought even more out of kilter, for reasons given in our Bible quotes above.

Now when Christians meet, one of the first questions is: "Where do you worship?" The women at this seemingly Christian newspaper hedged around with their answers. "Oh, we go where the spirit leads, wherever lively things are happening." That was the gist of their replies. This is not good enough. Christians need to know exactly who they are dealing with in situations like this. Besides, Pat and I have both been journalists for over thirty-five years. We don't accept vague replies; we want to get to the truth. So Pat persisted in questioning these people, to find out precisely what their religious background was. If I was to work with them in any way, which was in the back of my mind when we set out, knowing whether these were really "in the faith" was a necessity. They had already offered me the job of editor of their paper by this time, incidentally, an amazing development considering they had just met me and had no knowledge of my track record, references, etc.

After much prevarication, one of them said: "My father is a minister in the Reformed Church of Jesus Christ of Latter Day Saints and I have not repudiated the faith." This was the bottom line: The two leaders of the newspaper that we spoke with were both reformed Mormons. True, they visited Christian churches to get a charismatic buzz, but they had not repudiated the Mormon faith, which in the case of the Mormon offshoot they belonged to holds the ridiculous belief that Jesus Christ will return to earth to the town of Independence, Missouri. This belief is also held by the more numerous mainstream Mormons based in Salt Lake City. Don't hold your breath, Missourians, is my advice.

We spent an afternoon with the staff of this newspaper and while we were there representatives of true Christian organisations called in to leave news items. Some of the visitors were from "Jews for Jesus." Looking through back numbers we saw pictures of the

editorial staff being greeted by a wide assortment of American
Christian leaders, people like Pat Robertson of the 700 Club. It was
clear that none of these people had really looked into the background of this publication and its instigators. We were probably
the first people to find out the truth.

On our way out of Independence we lost our way and, I think,
led by God, we drove by the world headquarters of the Reformed
Mormons, who are separate from the Mormons of Salt Lake City.
There were vast edifaces filling up city blocks: this was no small,
poor organisation, but a major false religion with plenty of power,
money, and influence. The most shocking site of all was their worship centre, a mosque-like building, reflecting the Masonic roots of
Mormonism. It was a vast structure—it seemed as big as St. Paul's
Cathedral in London at the time, although this may have been a
false impression. Anyway, to us it looked ugly, unpleasant, and downright evil, like the false religion it represented.

We think that the whole set-up of this so-called Christian newspaper was Mormon-based and financed. It was run from a building owned and operated by Mormons. With the benefit of hind-
sight, the clues were all there. For example, in newspaper articles
church buildings were sometimes referred to as temples, a term
which a Christian would never use, but which would sound nor-
mal to a Mormon. There were other little giveaways: the Lord really opened our eyes and we left, never to make contact again.

The confusion between Mormonism and Christianity is spreading. A Christian leader and speaker we know booked into London's
newest hotel, only to find no Gideon Bible at his bedside. Instead
he found the Book of Mormon! He wrote a protest, pointing out
that many visiting American businessmen would be Christians and
they would find this offensive. He received a letter saying that
Gideon Bibles are on their way! The fate of the Mormon fiction is
unknown. A young man, a lapsed Sikh, visited us recently to record
a segment on a CD-ROM series on the world's religions. He too
mentioned Mormonism as a branch of Christianity, which it certainly is not. Recommended reading here is *The Godmakers* by Dave
Hunt which tells the whole truth about this oddball sect. Light

should have no fellowship with darkness and Christians should never enter into business with members of false sects—we are not to be unequally yoked. Similarly, churches should never get mixed up with the occult, something which leaders, pastors, and priests should be warning against, not encouraging.

Unfortunately, the standard of Bible study, or rather its absence, means that most churches in the West have no defence against the occult invasion and false doctrine of all kinds. Christians, even Christian leaders who one would hope would know better, are too ready to accept any manifestation of the supernatural as "a move of God." Thus we have the occult excesses of the Toronto Airport church, formerly the Vineyard, where people barked and growled and behaved in all manner of weird ways, only to be acclaimed as people "moving in the spirit." This is not biblical. God never demeans or degrades his people; they are not made fools of by the Holy Spirit. He does not require Christians to roll on the floor laughing like mad hyenas. He requires them to get to know our Lord by reading His word, although that, of course, does not at first seem so exciting.

The largest church in Aldershot, Hampshire, a place where our family worshipped for eight years, is just one of many in Britain to have gone way off base. A friend, a pastor from another church, looked in one night to see what they were up to. At that moment the old people had been told to pretend that they were jet planes and to run round the building with their arms out, screeching. Christian old people should behave with dignity, not like drunks who have lost their marbles. Perhaps they had been supping with "holy laughter" specialist Rodney Howard-Brown, who blasphemously styled himself the Holy Ghost's bartender. We should keep the faith, not the froth.

My former new age "guru" loved to con his way into churches, where gullible vicars allowed him to take so-called healing services. Dressed in fine robes, he could create quite a spectacle, with himself as the star. It was all quite sickening—but why was it allowed in the first place? Even as a naïve young man in my twenties I thought it a little odd, but what were professional, educated cler-

gymen doing allowing themselves to be hoodwinked like this? Their
training colleges have a lot to answer for.

I've just given you another little clue as to what's wrong in the
church as it staggers giggling into the twenty-first century. The
"guru," who loved ritualistic mumbo-jumbo, became master of the
local Masonic lodge. In many British lodges, the local vicar or
church sidesmen are also members. One of the most evil men I
knew, a person in the newspaper business who tried hard to bankrupt a small newspaper started by Pat and myself, was both a church
sidesman and a Mason. He was also a homosexual. Near the end of
his life we were amazed to see him go forward at the end of a
gospel service, praying to accept Jesus as his Savior. He told us
there were dark things in his life for which he needed forgiveness.
We just hope his conversion was genuine.

In America I know that the same Christian-Mason duality sometimes applies even to Baptist pastors who join the lodge in ignorance. So those who like to be seen to be "spiritual" reinforce each
other's false notions and assist each other into positions of power
and influence. They are "hoodwinked," a Masonic term which
means the applicant Mason's head is covered with a device called
a "hoodwink." Then, in a sick parody of the Christian new birth
experience, the new Mason is led from darkness into light at the
lodge meeting. Of course, Jesus tells us not to do things in secret
and to swear no oaths, and the first thing every new Mason does is
swear a bloodcurdling oath promising to preserve the dark secrets
of this satanic cult. The Bible simply tells us: "Let your yes be yes
and your no be no." That's not hard to remember, is it?

There are numerous books published revealing the secrets of
Freemasonry, but one simple test should tell the casual observer
something of the nature of this evil movement. Go to any Christian
church. In many of them, you can walk right in. Go along to a
service and you will, hopefully, be welcomed. At the least you will
be allowed to go in and take part. The buildings have windows and
you can glance in to see what goes on.

Now go along to your local Masonic lodge. First, you have to
find it. I worked as a senior journalist in different towns and cities

for many years without realising where the local lodges were, although they played a major if clandestine role in the civic life of those communities. The lodge is usually tucked up a back street, often with few if any markings telling what it is. The whole look of the place will almost certainly be hostile and unwelcoming. Keep-out notices might as well be placed on the gate, for this is the message. In fact, during meetings a man known as a Tyler is placed on the door to keep out the inquisitive. In Aldershot, Hampshire, England, the lodge took over a former church building and the first thing they did was to brick up all the windows. Inside it must be incredibly gloomy and unpleasant, with no air circulating, just the hot breath of the Masons reciting their litany of lies.

On certain days of the week you can see them scurrying along with their little cases full of regalia. They usually look grim and guilty—it doesn't look like they are having a lot of fun. Neither would you if you had to spend tens of hours learning all that ritual, to be spouted while wearing a funny little apron. I have never been to a Masonic meeting, as they are closed to outsiders, but I have been to near Masonic events, charity nights run by Masons which, it became clear to me, were very similar to some aspects of lodge meetings, after the formal, ritual part of the meeting was over. The emphasis was always on charity fundraising, but of a peculiar, unpleasant kind, in which participants tried to outdo each other with charitable bids, all very public and ostentatious.

Let's pause here and see what Jesus advised.

> And Jesus sat over against the treasury, and beheld how the people cast money into the treasury: and many that were rich cast in much. And there came a certain poor widow, and she threw in two mites, which make a farthing. And he called unto him his disciples, and saith unto them, Verily I say unto you, That this poor widow hath cast more in, than all they which have cast into the treasury: for all they did cast in of their abundance; but she of her want did cast in all that she had, even all her living.
>
> Mark 12:41–44

We are also to do our giving in secret, letting not our right hand know what our left is doing. Jesus was saying that those who make a big show of being charitable are earning no reward in heaven. Ostentatious charity does not impress God—it disgusts him.

Those Masons and city fathers shouting out their bids for auction items to impress each other are not a step nearer to heaven. "How hardly shall they that have riches enter into the kingdom of God! For it is easier for a camel to go through a needle's eye, than for a rich man to enter into the kingdom of God. And they that heard it said, Who then can be saved? And he said, The things which are impossible with men are possible with God" (Luke 18:24–27).

However hard we try, we will never be good enough. Not without God's grace and forgiveness, for which we must ask in the name of Jesus. Humility is something which comes hard to us all, particularly proud men, of which I was one. Dressing up in fancy costumes, so ridiculous that if the world and his wife saw they would burst out laughing, will not earn any brownie points with God.

Not that Christians should find Masonry amusing, for it is a more modern version of pagan mystery religions and is the world's largest secret society, a fraternal order for men in good standing, white men "sound of limb," although there are offshoots for men of colour and for women. So whereas Jesus came for everybody, including people of all races, the disabled, and women, Freemasonry is exclusive and excludes most people. All Masonic histories trace Masonry back to Eastern mystery religions, particularly those of Isis and Osiris of Egypt. Masonic authorities teach that these "pure" ancient religions were contaminated by Hebrews and then Christians and that Masonry is a means of rediscovering the ancient truths. Modern Masonry started in eighteenth century England, the first recorded meeting being in 1717 at a pub, or tavern—the Goose and Gridiron Tavern—in London. The first American lodges were chartered by the Grand Lodge of England, and the first U.S. lodge met in 1730 in Boston.

Tom C. McKenney, author of *The Deadly Deception* and *Please Tell Me*, two classic books exposing Freemasonry, estimates that there are between two and three million Masons in America and a million in the rest of the world. They are hugely influential and control much of the upper echelons of law enforcement, the judiciary, and the higher reaches of the armed forces. I recommend that you read Tom's books, published by Huntingdon House, to get the full picture of Masonic life. Suffice to say that it is satanic in origin and influence and that the ultimate secret of Freemasonry, revealed by Albert Pike, one of its former leaders, is that Satan is God! Masonic teaching is that Jesus and Satan are brothers, a claim echoed in Mormonism. Most people, even most Masons, have no knowledge of all this, thinking only of Shriners and their circus acts, the public display of Masonic "good works."

To become a Shriner you have to be a thirty-second degree Mason or Knight Templar. They are the "funsters" of Masonry, drinking a lot, having loud gatherings, and featuring vulgar, crude initiation ceremonies. They offset this, seemingly, by operating around twenty Shriners' hospitals in North America. "Helping crippled children" is their catchphrase. However, Tom McKenney quotes an *Orlando Sentinel* investigation in 1986 which showed that in the Florida Shrine as little as two percent of all the money collected in all their fundraising goes to building and operating hospitals. The rest went on things like entertainment, publicity, operating private bars and golf courses, travel and conventions, with $15.5 million spent on parties and conventions in 1986 alone.

I do not want to go too deeply into the Shrine, or Masonry at this stage, suffice to say I had a shock in 1998 when I discovered that my own "long lost" father was a member of both the Shrine and the Lutheran Church in Vancouver, Canada. He was unearthed by a chance inquiry, after many years in which I didn't know if he was dead or alive. I will tell you only that his attitude to me since has been anything but charitable or Christian. He started out by denying that I was his son and then, after much shilly-shallying, admitting that I could be, but blaming it all on my mother. She raised me after the war, having encountered him while he was a Canadian soldier stationed in Aldershot, Hampshire. She is adamant that he is indeed my father. Times were tough in Britain after the war, with rationing of all basic foodstuffs and widespread poverty, but my father never sent over so much as a can of beans. Nor

is he ever likely to, as his attitude is that he doesn't want to know
me. So much for the caring, charitable Shriners . . . Charitable
impulses cease, apparently, when their precious reputations are
threatened. A DNA test would settle the matter, but he has refused
to cooperate.

In these end times, when men are boastful and lovers of self,
there is almost never a charitable work which is done quietly, without fanfare or without someone wanting to claim credit. Hardly a
day passes in our newspaper office without the phone ringing and
a conversation similar to the following taking place: "Hello, we've
just raised XYZ pounds for charity and we wondered if you would
like to come round and take a photograph. We are presenting the
check to the (lucky recipient) on such and such a date." When we
politely state that we have no interest in taking pictures of people
waving large cheques around, they often get quite indignant, as if
the publicising of their good works was somehow part of their reward: "Look here, world—see how *good* we are."

Many of these fund-raising events are tacky in the extreme,
involving women going on sponsored walks for breast cancer chari-
ties wearing "decorated bras" or people sitting in shopping centres
in baths full of cold baked beans. There are non-stop drinking mara-
thons and boozy darts events held in pubs. Many are relatively harmless, but they all must be carried out in the spotlight of publicity to
have any validity, apparently. I often think this is the new religion
of Britain—ostentatious charity work, often involving fairly small
sums of actual money. When I referred to big cheques, I referred to
the physical size, as provided by the banks, not to the amount of
noughts on the end!

Quietly and with little fanfare, the people of God are going about
their work—as missionary doctors in Africa, taking supplies out to
the abandoned people of the Ukraine (where many are converting
to Christ), and helping the forgotten babies in Albanian orphan-
ages. Almost never does the national press, radio, or television report anything good about these true Christian heroes, but God notices what they are doing and they will get a great reward. Remember, the Bible tells us that the last will be first and the first last in

heaven, where the schoolteacher who, unseen and unheralded, helped little ones know the Lord may rank ahead of great ministries known to nations for their evangelism crusades. We must all beware of getting our rewards on earth, where men applaud our deeds, and concentrate instead on quietly pleasing God, so that our rewards are in heaven. God knows what is in our hearts and one day soon we will all stand before Him to give account of our lives.

At this ultimate moment of truth, no club members or relatives will be there to boost us, no medals or ribbons will decorate our chests, no titles will precede our names, only the one that matters to God: Sinner, saved by grace.

Chapter 6

Ecumenical Stew

The pope says the European Union is heaven-sent, so you know all is not right with it. Personally I think it was inspired from that other place.

Pope declares the EC is heaven sent

THE Roman Catholic Church has set the founding fathers of the European Community on the road to sainthood.

Some of us would say it is inspired by the other place! This is a British newspaper headline.

The Roman Catholic Church has set the founding fathers of the European Union on the path to sainthood. Catholic bishops have started the canonisation process for Konrad Adenauer, Alcide de Gasperi, and Robert Schuman, who are credited with devising the EU. The news came out of a synod for Europe in Rome and the Vatican press office confirmed that the canonisation process is underway.

Margaret Hebblethwaite of *The Tablet*, a Catholic newspaper, said that it was "extraordinary" for a politician to be canonised: "But the Pope is rather churning out the saints at the moment. The reason given was that these men founded the EC [European Community] on Roman Catholic principles." The *Daily Telegraph* quoted Chiara Lubich, a lay auditor at the synod, as saying: "The European Union is a design not only of human beings but of God." He added that the canonisation of the politicians would show that Europe was "built on a rock."

The pope made the first year of the new millennium the year of

WELCOME TO Pentecost 2000

on SUNDAY 11th JUNE 2000 at King George V Playing Field starting at 12pm to 7.30pm

Churches Together—an initiative which brought together all major British denominations for joint "Christian" celebrations.

unity, aimed at creating a Europe-wide united church, led by himself, of course. He is well on the way to achieving most of his aims before his death. Already all the main protestant denominations have made unity moves and "churches together" (an umbrella group for all denominations) held large open air Pentecost 2000 meetings in Britain at which all allegedly Christian denominations united. Meanwhile, the number two man in the Anglican/Episcopalian community, the Archbishop of York, went on an ecumenical trip to see the pope. He was accompanied by a Catholic bishop and the president of the Methodist Conference. Already an Anglican/Catholic commission has described the pope as "a gift to be received by all the churches" and, after five years of debate, the eighteen-member commission concluded that the Bishop of Rome had "a specific ministry concerning the discernment of truth" and accepted that only the pope had the moral authority to unite the various Christian denominations.

The millennium started with the pope and Dr. George Carey, Archbishop of Canterbury, making powerful pleas for the two churches to overcome their differences. The pope said that the twenty-two Christian leaders joining him in Rome would join him

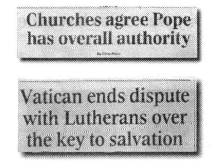

Churches agree Pope has overall authority

Vatican ends dispute with Lutherans over the key to salvation

Catholics and Jews agree to forge alliance

Newspaper headlines showing the march of the Catholic plan for a one-world church headed by the pope.

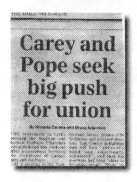

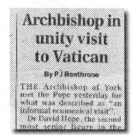

**Unity moves, reported in
London by the *Daily Telegraph*.**

in "asking forgiveness for the sins committed against Christian unity" during the past millennium. Dr. Carey proudly noted that he and Metropolitan Athanasios, of the Ecumenical patriarchate, had been singled out to help the pope push open a so-called holy door into the basilica of St.Paul's Without the Walls, part of a ceremony being held to mark Christian unity. The pope is counting on plenty of prayer support for his unity moves, for backing him in prayer is one of the ways Catholics can cut their time in purgatory, a place which has always been a useful and profitable invention of the Catholic church.

A revised list of indulgences, issued in time for the millennium penitents, said that a visit to one of Rome's major basilicas, combined with the recital of "special prayers for the intentions of the Pope," could get Catholic sinners a discount off their time in purgatory, an imaginary place where the Catholic church teaches that dead Catholics burn for their sins. The church has introduced a galaxy of different indulgences by which Catholics can reduce the time they will be tortured in purgatory. It's a lucrative business. The *Enchiridion Indulgentiarum*, better known as the *Manual of Indulgences*, also gives some spiritually correct ways to cut time in purgatory, such as praying ostentatiously in your office or giving up smoking and drinking alcohol. This would be tough for Catholics, particularly in America, where it is not unusual for the church basement to include a bar for Catholic social events. The booklet is one hundred fifteen pages long, written in Latin, and updating a previous document written in 1968 by Pope Paul VI.Watching TV broadcasts of the pope is recommended as a source of grace, while other suggestions include recommending foreign immigrants and orphan children for charitable donations. All of it has "saved by works" written all over it—a direct contradiction of the Bible, which makes it clear works will never be enough to please God!

Only faith in what Christ has done will get us to heaven and there will be no stopover at purgatory on the way. The penalty of our sins was paid in full at Calvary. Anyone who dies and finds themselves burning can abandon all hope, for there will be no escape, no remission, no time off, however many indulgences were earned in life and however many masses your relatives may be paying for. Christians, on the other hand, have not earned their salvation and every one of us will go straight into the presence of their Saviour, for to die is to be present with the Lord and the moment of our death is precious in His sight. Death has totally lost its sting if you believe in the Lord Jesus. If you still have any fear of death, you must get some good basic Bible teaching to reassure you, for the Lord does not want you to be afraid.

In the Christian newsletter *Contending Earnestly for the Faith*, the Anglicans' Dr. Carey is reported as saying: "In a world torn apart by violence and division, Christians need urgently to be able to speak with a common voice, confident of the authority of the gospel of peace." This excellent Christian publication, in its edition of September 1999, went on to comment:

> It is in fact the authority of the gospel and the whole Word of God which has in the past prevented Bible-believing Christians from being able to speak with a common voice with the Roman Catholic church. Rome's history is one of suppression of the truths of the Gospel and their replacement with a religious system which bound people up with dead works in the vain attempt to earn salvation and brought them into submission to a corrupted clergy.

Brave and brilliant words. Not many religious writers in Europe today would dare say as much even though many know it to be true.

The pope has also been wooing the Muslims and I have a pic-

ture of him kissing the Koran at a
meeting with them. Under the picture
in the magazine: *Contending Earnestly
for the Faith*, April 2000 edition, the
caption states: "At the end of an audience with Patriarch Raphael I of Iraq
the Pope bowed to the Muslim holy
book, the Qu'ran, presented to him by
the delegation, and kissed it as a sign

A Christian magazine pictures the pope
kissing the Koran.

of respect." A sign of the times indeed! The Muslims should beware, because the agenda of the Roman Catholic Church is non-
negotiable and a Vatican Council document on ecumenism states

A report from the *Financial Times*
showing the pope making some Islamic
contacts.

that dialogue is not an end in itself.
Rather it "aims at preparing the way
for their unity of faith in the bosom of
a church one and visible." In the same
Christian journal is a picture of the
pope sitting at an altar in Israel before an upside-down cross. Those who
know the occult will realise that this

is a blasphemous mockery of the cross of Christ. The picture was,
at the time of writing, available at *www.ewtn.com/holyland2000/
gallery/gallery6.asp#*. The caption reads: "Pope John Paul II sitting
at an altar in Korazim, Israel." The backdrop depicts Christ with
an open book that reads: "Love your enemies, I will come soon."

Why an upside-down cross? Some say it is a sign of martyrdom
as Peter was crucified upside down. However, the occult dictio-
nary claims that the inverted cross is a blasphemy or mockery of
the Christian cross. As someone who once dabbled in the occult,
and whose stock of books on magic and mysticism was burned by
my wife when she became a Christian, I can confirm that this is
true. Odd that this thought had not occurred to the pope.

Despite his age and infirmity this world travelling pope pushed
the unity agenda with great determination after inaugurating "The
Jubilee Holy Year" on the eve of the millennium. He visited Egypt
in February to meet Coptic Pope Shenusa III, the first time a Catho-

lic pope had ever visited this Arab Coptic Christian community. There are seven million Coptic Christians in Egypt. In March it was the turn of the Jews when, after apologising for the "sins" of Christians, he visited Bethlehem to be welcomed by Yasser Arafat and to "deplore" the so-called "plight" of the Palestinians. The pope went on to the Holocaust Memorial before delivering his own Sermon on the Mount. After visiting Jerusalem in March, begging forgiveness from the Jews, and appealing for Christian unity in a mass at the Church of the Holy Sepulchre, the pope prayed at the Wailing Wall and called for a fresh start at the shrine of Jesus' resurrection. Israeli commentators hailed all this showboating as the start of a new, conciliatory era. The truth is that the pope has long wanted to have control of Jerusalem, a possible future headquarters of the one-world religion he is trying to establish.

Conor Cruise O'Brien, an Irish historian with close Vatican contacts, says the pope had a dream that he would see a sign from God heralding an age of religious renewal across the earth. According to O'Brien, writing in the *Daily Telegraph*, the pope is contemplating some kind of alliance with Islamic leaders "so that the religious of the world will be united for a final victory over the irreligious." O'Brien explained that the pope hoped for "a coalition of all faiths agreeing to differ on many things but combining to oppose abortion, contraception, and divorce." There are many instances of this happening already in Western countries, with Catholics and evangelicals uniting to form pressure groups with the "Christian Coalition" in America and "Life" in Britain. Some good does come of this but it also tends to blur the clear scriptural differences of doctrine between believers in true and apostate churches. We should always remember that it was the "religious" people who gave Jesus so much trouble during His ministry and finally succeeded in having Him killed. There is a big difference between "religion" and Bible-based Christianity.

Already the Vatican has ended its dispute with many Lutherans over the key to salvation and they have come to an accord described as a milestone in ecumenical efforts. The Lutheran World Federation has settled its differences with the Catholics over how man can achieve salvation. A joint Catholic/Lutheran commission of theologians has been working since 1967 to resolve outstanding differences and has declared that man is saved "by the grace of God." It adds that faith and good works are granted by the grace of God, so you are saved by a little bit of faith and some works, it seems.

Cardinal Edward Cassidy, chairman of the Pontifical Council for Christian Unity, described the accord as a milestone in ecumenical efforts to end differences with the world's sixty-six million Lutherans. He added: "The consensus will be of importance not only for Catholic/Lutheran relations and future dialogue, but also for progress in the search for unity between Catholics and other communities coming out of the Reformation controversies." Apparently the new accord settles all the insults that the two sides have hurled at each other since the sixteenth century. The decision means that "where such consensus has been reached, the condemnations levelled at one another in the sixteenth century no longer apply to the respective partner today," according to the cardinal, who added: "We cannot, of course, erase these condemnations from history. We can, however, now state that in so far as a consensus on the understanding of basic truths articulated in the joint declaration has been achieved, the corresponding condemnations found in the Lutheran Confession and the Council of Trent no longer apply." Readers should note that not all Lutherans agree: members of the International Lutheran Council have opposed the decision.

Despite poor health, the pope's pace didn't let up in 2001, when he went on a journey to Greece, Syria, and Malta, his ninety-third overseas excursion. In the footsteps of the Apostle Paul he went to Damascus, Syria, where he became the first pope to pray inside an Islamic holy place, the Unmayed Mosque which was a Christian church until the seventh century Arab conquest. His visit to Greece didn't go so well, for fringe groups demonstrated against the man they called "antichrist." The Orthodox churches are suspicious of Catholic designs on their East European flocks, and their hostility dates from the Great Schism of 1054, when Eastern and Western Christianity split. Not a single black-robed orthodox priest greeted the pope as he stepped off his plane at Athens airport. His next plan was a visit to Russia to attempt to heal divisions with the Russian Orthodox Church.

No Christian has any excuse for not knowing what the Catholic church really believes and how it regards all other branches of Christianity as worthless. In September 2000 the Vatican-approved document *Dominus Iesus* was published. It was drawn up by Cardinal Joseph Ratzinger, head of the Congregation for the Doctrine of the Faith, which is what they call the Inquisition today. Ratified by the pope, it stated, in part: "There exists a single church of Christ, which subsists in the Catholic Church governed by the Successor of Peter and by the bishops in communion with him." Other churches are "not churches in the proper sense." These "separated churches and communities suffer from defects. . . ." Churches which fail to hail the pope as head and follow his dictates "are not churches in the proper sense." This breathtaking arrogance from

Not all churches are equal, seemingly, as this report in the *Times* (London) revealed.

the church whose golden cup is "full of abominations" (Revelation 17:4). The Church of Rome in effect says it is the way, the truth, and the life—you must come to God by us.

The key word in the religious world today is "interfaith." The new millennium started in Britain with the leaders of nine faiths "standing together" at the Palace of Westminster, the building that is home to Britain's two houses of parliament. This is how *Times'* religion correspondent Victoria Combe reported the event:

All faiths together in the House of Lords (*Daily Telegraph* report).

Leaders from the nine religious faiths in Britain stood together in the Palace of Westminster and made a public commitment to "work together for the common good" in the third millennium.

News Bulletin

Church seeks multi-faith representation in Lords

It was the Church of England bishops who asked the British government for leaders of non-Christian faiths to be given seats in the country's second chamber, the House of Lords.

The unprecedented event, hosted by the Prime Minister, brought together Christians, Muslims, Hindus, Buddhists, Jews, Sikhs, Jains, Baha'is and Zoroastrians in the Royal Gallery of the House of Lords. The Archbishop of Canterbury, Dr. George Carey, stood shoulder to shoulder with the Chief Rabbi, Dr. Jonathan Sacks, the secretary general of the Muslim Council of Great Britain, Iqbal Sacranie, and leaders of the other faiths.

The writer describes their colourful mixture of turbans, cassocks, skullcaps, and saffron robes—some might call it an unholy stew! Their pledge was to build a better society, "grounded in values and ideals we share," and to work together "to help bring about a better world now and for generations to come." At least they didn't promise to do what the Mormons do and baptise the dead! Prime Minister Tony Blair, a great interfaith man, said the occasion was "progress of a very special sort" for Britain and showed how religions which had often been cause for division—which is putting it mildly—"can reach out across the divide." The divide between the true faith and the false religions, Mr. Blair? I think not. The Lord our God is a jealous God. He doesn't approve of idol worshippers. Some people do see through phoney "Saint" Tony, despite his unctuous "pulpit manner"—he even launched his 2001 re-election campaign while waving a hymnbook in front of school-children at a school assembly. Daniel Johnston, in an article in the *Daily Telegraph* of December 12, 2000, castigated Blair and his crew for sanctioning the "morning after" pill—a form of early abortion—and "spare part" cloning and said it confirmed Labor's secularist agenda. Blair votes in favour of abortion at Westminster. Daniel Johnston asks how long before Britain follows the Dutch in legalising the killing of hospital patients. While secular writers are raising these questions of morality, where are our church leaders and what issues do they consider important? An MP friend of mine said that at pre-election public meetings run by the local council of churches he was usually quizzed on "the environment," the new holy writ.

The Anglicans' Dr. Carey, always ready with an appropriately wet word for the occasion, said that while the millennial celebrations were Christian in nature, he acknowledged "the increasingly important contribution of other faiths." He concluded: "This event will, I believe, be seen by future generations as truly historic." Historically wrong, I am afraid, Archbishop. This is just part of the great build-up to the one-world church. When Antichrist crashes on to the scene, the whore church will be his spiritual sidekick, headed by the false prophet—perhaps the pope of the day. But after three and a half years the whore church will be smashed forever, by its supposed ally, Antichrist. This is when Rome, the city on seven hills, will be destroyed in a day, as the Bible predicts. So make the most of your moment of glory, Dr. Carey. You haven't got long to enjoy it.

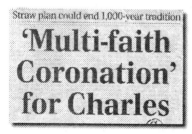

Straw plan could end 1,000-year tradition

'Multi-faith Coronation' for Charles

There are plans to make the coronation of Charles as the next (last?) king of Britain a "multi-faith" affair.

The main pointer to what's ahead in Britain is the plan for Prince Charles to have a multi-faith coronation. In the immediate aftermath of the September 2001 attacks on America, he met Osama Bin Laden's brother and stressed his support for Islam, being pictured in Islamic headgear. Charles even has an Islamic garden at his home! Although the constitutional role of the monarch in Britain includes headship of the Church of England and the title Defender of the Faith, which is what the queen is supposed to be, Charles has already stated that he intends only to be "Defender of Faith." He no longer regards Christianity as "the faith," a result of the unfortunate influence on him of oddball mystics like the late Laurens van der Post, who subsequent to his death has been exposed as a charlatan and fantasy artist.

Britain's coronation ceremony, traditionally held in Westminster Abbey, has been a Christian event since A.D. 973, when Edgar was crowned by Archbishop Dunstan at Bath. At the coronation of the present queen in 1953, she pledged to "preserve inviolably the settlement of the Church of England." However, her multi-faith son, who talks to trees as well as Hindus, wants his coronation—if it ever occurs—to reflect the other religions now practised in Britain. A report by the then home secretary, Jack Straw, says the establishment of the Church of England causes "religious disadvantage" to other faiths and Christian denominations. In her coronation oath, the queen swore to uphold the protestant faith, but this too may no longer be appropriate in so-called "multicultural Britain," something which is far more evident in reports from left-wing politicians and politically correct newspapers and broadcasting bodies than it is on the ground in Britain, where comfortably more than three-quarters of the population would still happily describe themselves as Christian, if asked.

The report, a Home Office paper, questions the sovereign's role as Supreme Governor of the Church of England and Defender of the Faith. Senior figures in the Labour government think other religions should have a larger role in public life. The report, by Professor Paul Weller and a team from Derby University, says the next coronation could be a focus of controversy and adds: "The religious composition of society has changed significantly since the last coronation and the next coronation will therefore highlight a series of very important issues and complexities." Of course, what these intelligent men, high in IQs and low in wisdom, don't know is that a nation which turns its face from the one true God is doomed. God has stepped in on many occasions to preserve Britain, which for hundreds of years has sent missionaries round the world. The nation prayed—and was saved, at crucial times even in recent history, like the Battle of Britain and, before that, the evacuation from Dunkirk, an incredible modern miracle in which the often stormy English Channel was quelled while thousands of little boats scurried back and forth to Normandy to rescue our army from the beaches.

Sixty years ago, at the height of the Blitz, firebombs rained down on London and other big British cities. The whole of London seemed blood-red as the Germans aimed to "take out" the entire city of London, hub of the capital. On one night alone, December 29, 1940, one hundred thirty-six German bombers dropped ten thousand incendiaries, aimed at setting the heart of the city ablaze. In the middle of it all was St. Paul's Cathedral, considered by many to be the spiritual hub of the United Kingdom. Aware of its symbolic significance, Prime Minister Winston Churchill had given orders that the cathedral was to be saved at all costs. More importantly, the people of Britain prayed to God for help.

Anne Walcot, then a twenty-eighty–year–old bookkeeper for a firm on Ludgate Hill, at the foot of St. Paul's Churchyard, was firewatching with a friend. As fires flared everywhere and glass shattered, this is how Anne, now a widow of eighty-eight, recalls the scene: "People were kneeling on the pavement and weeping as they prayed for God to save St. Paul's." The people's prayers were answered: Britain was then basically a God-fearing country where our Lord was not mocked and morality ruled. With Britain under threat again, how many of the people have God to turn to? God will not look kindly on a nation which plays the whore with other gods. He is a jealous God. And one way in which a nation is judged is by being handed over to her enemies. As I write this Britain is about to lose its sovereignty to the new European superstate . . .

Prince Charles, sometimes called the clown prince because of his numerous idiotic notions, such as talking to his plants, loses no opportunity to boost false religions. If there is a Sikh temple, there he is in prayer pose, garlanded with flowers and talking about tolerance. Many of us British Christians think we are the tolerant ones, not only putting up with but paying him handsomely for all this nonsense. When he went along to the gala festival to celebrate

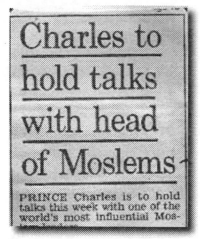

Prince Charles—all things to all religions.

the three hundredth anniversary of the founding of the Khalsa, the Sikh Brotherhood, he told the audience of four thousand:

> Sikhism teaches, and Sikhs aspire, to tolerance, a willingness to stand up and be counted, a repudiation of discrimination on grounds of caste and race. This anniversary should be celebrated not only by Sikhs but also by all of us who long to live in a saner world where the truth is recognised of Guru Nanak's teaching that "God's light pervades every creature and every creature is contained in this light."

Charles is rather promiscuous in his religious life, as he also thinks there is much to praise in Islam. He has held talks with one of the world's most influential Moslem leaders. His decision to receive the Sheik of Al-Azhar, the spiritual head of the Sunni Moslems, was said to underline his commitment to deepening his ties with Islam. The Sheik, Dr. Muhammed Savyid Tantawi, is head of the Al Azhar University in Cairo, Egypt, and was on a six-day visit to Britain at the invitation of—who else—Archbishop of Canterbury George Carey, a man who seems to lose no opportunity to advance false religion in Britain. A report in the *Daily Mail*, London, said:

> Charles, who sometimes in private wears a Moslem djellaba [a long flowing Arabic garment], has been criticised by Christian

groups for his failure to criticise Islamic human rights abuses and persecution of Christians. At the end of the month he is to host a dinner at St. James's Palace for the Oxford Centre for Islamic Studies, which has provoked powerful opposition to its plan to build a 108 foot minaret in the heart of the city.

Just in case we have missed the multi-faith message, the government is planning to make it legal for a Catholic to be crowned in Britain. Ministers of Tony Blair's government plan to support a proposal to allow the monarch to be a Roman Catholic or to marry a member of that faith. This would raise interest-

The queen, head of the Church of England, pays homage to the pope. From the *Times* of London.

ing questions about the role of the "established church," the Church of England, over which the monarch is titular head. Plans to change the law are expected to be tabled in the House of Lords, Britain's upper chamber, to amend the Act of Settlement of 1701 which prevents a Catholic from succeeding to the throne of Great Britain. The act also bars the heir to the throne from marrying a member of the Roman Catholic Church, although in the case of Charles there is little sign that he intends to marry his mistress.

A report in the *Daily Telegraph* in November 1999 quoted a government spokesman as saying: "Tony Blair is against discrimination, including bias against Roman Catholics. He is married to a Catholic and his children are brought up Catholics." Cardinal Winning, Scotland's most senior Catholic, has called for changes to be made to the act and several Church of England bishops support changes to the coronation ceremony, not just to allow Catholics in, but to involve other religions as well!

The Act of Settlement was designed to ensure a Protestant line of monarchs in the aftermath of the "glorious revolution" that saw the Catholic James replaced by William and Mary of Orange, from Holland. Currently the heir to the throne can marry any protestant. As the Anglican church has declined in Britain, so the Catholic church has grown in influence, with most of the leading "moral commentators" in national newspapers speaking from a Roman Catholic viewpoint. More Catholics attend church than Anglicans for the first time since the Reformation in Britain. Figures in the *Catholic Directory* show that on average 1,086,268 attended Mass in 1997, compared to 815,500 at Church of England services. Anglican church attendance has declined by an average of two percent a year since the 1960s. In 1994 there were 1.4 million Anglicans in Britain. The Catholic church has also lost worshippers, but not at such a rapid rate. In 1995 there were 1,135,047 Catholics at Sunday services throughout the country.

It is in schools that the mix n' match and merger of religion into one vast, incomprehensible world religion is proceeding apace. I was sent this press release from Sandhurst School in the Royal County of Berkshire. It is headed:"Commonwealth Date" and describes a trip which four pupils and a teacher took to Westminster Abbey, London, for the Commonwealth Celebration Day Ceremony. The Commonwealth is the association of countries, almost a third of the world's nations, which all have in common the fact that they were once British colonies. The main guests at the abbey were the queen and Prince Charles, together with the prime minister and other politicians.

This is what the press release says: "The theme of the day was the communication challenge and relevant teachings were read out by members of the six major world religions. The flags of the Commonwealth countries were carried through the abbey and the audience was entertained by a steel band and traditional Nigerian dancing. . . . We were introduced to Prince Charles, Mr. and Mrs. Blair and Kofi Anan, the UN Secretary General." Please note that I am not criticising the school, its teachers, or pupils. I just find it interesting that it is taken for granted these days that these major international events have to be "interfaith." It certainly wasn't like that in the days of the British Empire, when God used the opportunity to send Christian missionaries to every colony, thus using an empire to spread the word in much the same way as the Roman Empire was used in the first century.

Today it would not be possible to do this. We would have to send "multi-faith" missions which would be such a moral muddle that they would achieve nothing. Yet the "all roads lead to God" lie is being remorselessly drummed into our young people. Let me quote from a press release from Surrey County Council, headed "World religions capture classroom interest," dating back to April 16, 1996. This is what it proudly states:

> Developing pupils' interest in religion and preparing them for life in a multi-cultural world is the aim of Surrey County Council's exciting new religious education syllabus. The new syllabus, which will be taught in all Surrey schools, will introduce pupils from five to 16 to Christianity and other world religions to help them understand and appreciate their own religious traditions and cultural diversity.
>
> Until now, five and seven year old pupils learnt exclusively about Christianity and the study of other religions was not common until secondary school. Under the new syllabus, these pupils will continue to learn about Christianity, but will also be introduced to aspects of Islam and Judaism. From the age of seven aspects of Hinduism will also be introduced and when pupils move into secondary school they will also begin to learn about Buddhism and Sikhism. As they progress through school pupils will also be encouraged to look at religious attitudes to economics, art, language, history and music. By the time they leave Surrey schools, pupils will have gained an understanding of not only Christianity but also the five other principal faiths represented in the UK today.

Education policy officer David Hall said:

> We think it is vital for Surrey pupils to be equipped to live in a multi-cultural, multi-faith world. Learning about a diversity of religions from a young age will teach pupils to respect and empathise with other cultures and at the same time ensure their awareness of the special place of Christianity within this country.

The syllabus is not just concerned with developing knowledge and understanding of Christianity and the other faiths, but is also about encouraging pupils to think deeply about their own issues regarding life in the world today.

And so it waffles on, full of trendy cliches and multicultural mush. I believe that children "educated" in such a manner will end up like the baffled readers of a *Guardian* leader article (the *Guardian* is Britain's leading leftie newspaper). Basically, they will be in a complete muddle and need to run round the park a couple of times to clear their brains.

For a start, it is not true that Britain is "multi-faith." This is particularly so in prosperous, white, mainly middle-class Surrey, my home county, where just a tiny percentage of the population would be anything other than "nominal Christian." It must also be remembered that many immigrants are born-again Christians, particularly those from the West Indies. In London over half the Sunday attendance at Christian churches is non-white. If some of the so-called education experts ever tripped over a church doorway and stumbled inside, they would see that their idea of pandering to immigrants by pushing non-Christian religions is not wanted by a large percentage of the immigrants themselves. It is wrong to even assume that all Asians are of "other religions." As Tom Chacko, of the Alliance of Asian Christians, says, there are around thirty thousand Asian Christians in Britain today.

In March 1960, I was at a school run by Surrey County Council's education committee, which in those days was run by sensible men. Along with every other pupil in Surrey I was presented with a King James Bible. Not a "multi-faith statement," but the inspired Word of the living God.

This is what it says on the inscription inside the cover: "Alan Franklin: the Surrey Education Committee present you with this book, the most valuable thing this world affords, desiring that you use it whilst at school and retain it when you leave. Herein is wisdom which will lead you to all truth, provide comfort and guidance and teach you the whole duty of man." Signed, Robert Cross, headmaster. Mr. Cross frequently had to live up to his name with me, for I was not a good boy but, I am ashamed to have to confess, a troublemaker. I had no intention of ever reading the Bible, but being raised "never to look a gift horse in the mouth" I took it home anyway.

Somehow that book survived countless moves, big upheavals in my life, good times, bad times, wicked times, drunken times. While I became a rock group drummer it stayed somewhere gathering dust on some obscure shelf in my bedroom. Through two marriages it somehow trailed along with me, still unopened and unread. Twenty-one years passed, years that in many ways I would like to forget. My second wife, amazingly and to my complete astonishment, suddenly started reading my old Bible and became a Christian! It lit up Pat's life. It has since lit up mine. We still read it. It is in front of me as I write this book and I am quoting from it as I go. As a child I was not "raised up in the way I should go." My family was ignorant of Christ. I met no Christians that I know of, certainly nobody witnessed to me as I grew up.

The only man I knew for sure was a churchgoer was a cruel teacher who beat me every day. When we were dragged along to a musty old local church for some school ceremonial, it meant nothing to me other than a trip out of school. But the life of God is in His Word. That was why it was—and still is—so important to give Bibles to young people, so vital that they are given a grounding in the Word, so necessary that they are taught the clear truth of the gospel, not some pagan mish-mash which will probably leave them thinking all religion is equally boring and ridiculous, if they remember anything at all of these odd lessons they get today.

My Bible was a time bomb of truth waiting to explode into our lives. Make sure your children and all their friends are given the Word of the Lord, so that they may one day have a chance to find out the truth for themselves. We can no longer rely on schools, churches, or any other institution to teach Christianity in a coherent way. The only place left for many of us, whose churches have gone peculiar or apostate, is the home. Here we can still pass on the truth of that "old, old story." Even this may come under attack soon, so act now, while the light can still shine in this dark old world of sin.

Chapter 7

The Rulers of Blunderland

Steel, glass, and power—the European Union's main headquarters in Brussels, Belgium.

On my first visit to the European Parliament, it struck me as a parliament of fools. It consists of people who have no power, who are merely tolerated and paid attendance allowances, rather like overfed pets. They are certainly overfed: the restaurants of Brussels, Belgium, and Strasbourg, France, wax fat on the expense accounts of Eurocrats and MEPs. However, the more intelligent soon realise that behind the webs of fine words, they are wasting their time. There only to make a pretence of democracy, they vainly press their little plastic voting buttons, often they know not what for.

The very name deceived British voters. At first it was the innocuous sounding Common Market. Then it became the more officious sounding EEC, European Economic Community. Suddenly we found ourselves living in the EU, the European Union, which has the ominous ring of a deal out of which you cannot get. A union is easy to get into, whether it's marriage or anything else involving legal contracts. Getting out may not be possible at all, and to even try to escape may carry a hefty price tag. There is no better example than America's terrible Civil War. The southern states were not allowed out of the union once they were in and were comprehensively flattened when they tried to secede.

If Alice in Wonderland was made ruler of Blunderland, this is what it would be like. The following is all true, unfortunately:

- Euroland has attempted to ban everything it doesn't like, from the British double-decker bus to the prawn cocktail flavoured-potato chip, not to mention the pound sterling.
- Euroland hired a horde of sniffer dogs to smell dung, to help Eurocrats decide how smelly Europe's smelliest farmyard could be.
- Euroland tried to get snails reclassified as fish in order that snail farmers could get better subsidies under the Common Fisheries Policy.
- Euroland declared that carrots were fruit, on the grounds that they could be used to make preserves.

Euroland accuses British journalists of making up silly stories about the superstate, to put people off it. We say they do a pretty good job of looking stupid without any help from us. In early 2001 an EU directive reclassified flowerpots as packaging, instantly putting up the price of every pot plant. Even worse are orders like the Seeds Directive which bans the buying or selling of less popular seeds.

Unless vegetable cultivars are on national lists, buying or selling them is illegal, putting at risk both choice of vegetables and genetic diversity. It is also a gross infringement of civil liberty and another example of how the Brussels dictators cannot resist interfering in every aspect of Europeans' lives. What could be more harmless, after all, than a willing seller selling to a willing buyer seeds of Webbs Wonderful Lettuce or Scarlet Emperor string beans —two traditional varieties now doomed under the new regime, as it costs too much for seedsmen to maintain less popular varieties on the official "list." How strange and sinister that in the brave new world your favorite beans are banned.

The strangest thing of all is that the EU has two headquarters, one in Brussels, Belgium and one in Strasbourg, France. For three weeks of every month Europe is governed from Brussels. Then hundreds of trucks arrive to transport the whole kit and kaboodle hundreds of miles (or should I say kilometres) to Strasbourg for the fourth week. At the end of the fourth week, back come those trucks to haul the whole crazy mess back to Brussels. For the trucking firm owners it must be the most incredible stroke of luck as they go round and round the merry-go-round twelve times a year to the jolly tune of: "It's only taxpayers' money."

Why have two capitals, you might ask. The USA seems to manage pretty well with just one little old capitol, Washington, D.C., but then Americans do not have to pacify the French. When the European Union was set up, they had to be very careful about the choice of a capital and Brussels was chosen as a neutral sort of place for the headquarters. This did not please the French, who dug their heels in and demanded that it be located there, hence the Alice-in-Wonderland style compromise.

Never mind, the Euro taxpayers can always be relied upon to stump up. The ironic thing is that probably not one percent of them even know all this, so ignorant are people of what it going on. The press simply does not focus on these things and the only people who find out the truth are the ones who assiduously read the more boring-looking pages of the serious newspapers.

The two centres are rivals and illustrate the follies of Euro excess. France tried to lock the Union into its borders by building an enormous, ill-planned building in Strasbourg—the one with the Tower of Eurobabel as its centrepiece. This monumental pile is full of see-through structures, supposedly to illustrate the theme of parliamentary transparency, an ideal to which the organisation is allegedly devoted, except when it comes to items like personal expenses and contracts to relatives.

The hypocrisy of this was shown in the summer of 2000, when many of the MEPs were away on holiday. The European political establishment, the unelected commissioners and EU ambassadors, took their chance to slip in a whole series of new secrecy laws, aimed at making sure journalists, never mind the voters, have little chance of finding out what they are up to. The sweeping new secrecy laws will curb the public's right to know details of talks on military, security, and foreign policy matters. Things like drugs and immigration could also be covered by the restrictions, say campaigners for freedom of information.

This new code of access to documents, which became law at the end of August, 2000, was rushed through under something called a "written procedure." This prevents debate by members. It was agreed by ambassadors, with only four member states of fifteen voting against, at the request of Javier Solana, an ex-NATO secretary-general who is the EU's first head of foreign policy—another sign that what we have here is a state, not a confederation. The EU can now withhold information on "public security, the security and defence of the union or of its member states, military or non military crisis management, international relations, monetary stability, court proceedings, inspections and investigations."

This secrecy bombshell is in direct contradiction to a promise in the Amsterdam Treaty to enshrine the public's right of access to EU documents and goes against repeated pledges of more "transparency" in decision making. The excuse for this creep toward dictatorship is that the rules are necessary to support moves toward common defence and foreign policies. However, they also cover the plan to set up an EU paramilitary police force, initially five thousand strong, and a sixty thousand personnel rapid reaction force, which could be used to quell "violence, armed conflicts and massive population movements."

The secrecy clampdown was rushed through despite protests from Jacob Soderman, the European ombudsman, who said the new secrecy laws would apply to areas now open to public scrutiny. British civil liberties group Statewatch complained that the new rules were rushed through "when the institutions in Brussels were half empty." It added that the new rules would "impinge in a major way on the EU civil as distinct from the military practices." Some EU countries which are used to open government, like the Scandinavian states, are reportedly upset at the move.

It is clear from the censorship and stealthy formation of squads of riot troops that someone, somewhere in the heart of the EU, sees trouble ahead and is preparing to rule with an iron fist. A contingent of riot police, with their vehicles, is permanently on standby a short distance from the parliament building, as for some reason those inside are not completely sure of their great popularity with the people who pay their bills! Incidentally, after one riot by peasant farmers, the order was given to concrete over the cobbles, so

Threat of anti-euro uprisin

Anti-EU protestors were among those protesting at an EU summit in Sweden in June 2001.

that citizens wishing to pass a direct comment on their love for the Eurocrats could not prise them out of the ground and use them as handy missiles! The first visit of President George W. Bush to Europe to meet EU leaders, in June 2001, was marked by the worst riots Sweden had seen in seventy years, much of them directed in impotent fury against "globalisation" and the emerging EU super-

EU calls for an iron fist to crush the summit protesters

The EU's reaction was to promise an "iron fist" crackdown in future—shades of things to come.

state. Newspapers spoke of anti EU riots—a harbinger of things to come, particularly with the introduction of the unpopular euro in 2002 pushing prices up at a stroke. Next came an ominous headline saying that the EU was planning to use "an iron fist" against future demonstrators.

So are we looking at the real reason Europe needs a sixty thousand strong "rapid reaction force," comprising the cream of the British, French, German, and other continental armies? Rapid reaction to what? Internal repression is the name of the game here, as those who wake up one day and find their freedom gone may turn uppity, although draconian gun control legislation in countries like Britain greatly reduces our opportunity to fight for freedom. Another cunning, long planned move by the New World Order, one-world government advocates. Watch out America, you are next for personal disarmament, perhaps in the guise of "preventing terrorism."

No sooner had I written the above than I saw that British en-
thusiasm for rapid reaction forces didn't end in Europe. On September 4, 2000, Britain tabled proposals for a standing United
Nations rapid reaction force. These proposals went before the Millennium Summit, a gathering designed to flesh out many of the
plans for world government and ratify hundreds of international
treaties, giving United Nations bodies the right to interfere in nations around the globe. British foreign secretary Robin Cook said
he would like to see a British-based UN
staff college and an "on-standby" headquarters for "UN peacekeeping forces"
which would be able to coordinate
rapid deployment to the world's
trouble spots. Britain also has a world
famous officer-training facility at
Sandhurst, Berkshire, where thousands of officers for Commonwealth
and third world nations as well as the
British Army are trained. Slotting in a
UN staff college alongside would be
easy—the infrastructure is all there.

This is how a green magazine satirized the
UN forces in action. The caption reads: "Be
peaceful or we'll kill you!"

In the past, putting together UN missions has been a fraught
and time-consuming process, with many arguments about man-
dates and whose forces should be used. This move would short-cut
all that. The danger here is that whereas in the past UN operations
have been the subject of debate, having a ready-made force to hand
could mean them being deployed before anyone has been able to
put the brakes on. British forces are widely regarded by experts as
the world's best and, although the professional army is small, it is
highly effective, well trained, and particularly air-mobile. In recent operations in Sierra Leone it was said that one thousand British paratroopers were more effective than the previous deployment
of ten thousand assorted troops from countries like Nigeria, India,
and Jordan. A British-led force would put the backbone into a UN
army, which, as someone who believes in the nation state, is the
last thing I would want.

Furthermore, this revolutionary move was made with no discussion in the British parliament and few stories in the British press. One person who got wind of what was going on was the veteran Socialist Tony Benn, who although a Labour MP until the June 2001 election and formerly a senior government minister, is no friend of the present Blair administration, which is run on spin doctoring and mirrors. He said the UN army move was a "secretly negotiated policy" which had never been debated in Parliament.

British foreign secretary Robin Cook in August 2000 published plans for an international criminal court and even asked opposition parties to give the legislation a smooth ride through Parliament. Britain has been one of the leading proponents of an international criminal court since it was approved by more than one hundred countries in a treaty in 1998. The court would have jurisdiction over war crimes, genocide, and crimes against humanity and would be set up under UN auspices. Foreign Office minister Peter Hain, formerly a leading member of the Campaign for Nuclear Disarmament, described the new court as "a vital international mechanism to ensure that dictators, torturers, and oppressors around the world cannot do what they like with impunity, but are brought to justice." The Clinton administration supported the establishment of the international court in principle. However, the Pentagon is worried that U.S. personnel could fall victim to politically motivated cases brought before the court.

While it sounds reasonable to want to bring despots to justice, it is highly likely that the real world despots, the repressive Chinese leadership, for example, which imprisons and tortures thousands of Christians, while running slave labour camps for those

ETHICAL FOREIGN POLICY OPPOSITION SUPPORT SOUGHT FOR PUSHING LEGISLATION THROUGH PARLIAMENT

Cook moves to back world criminal court

Moves to establish a world criminal court are well under way.

who object, would never face justice. Who would have the guts to
take them on, and their 2,500,000-strong army? No, the big fish
won't swim in this court. It would instead be used to bend the will
of little countries to do the UN's bidding. It may be international,
but there won't be much justice there, just another means of breaking down the nation state.

One person who recognised too late that this was exactly what
the European Union was about was former British prime minister
Margaret Thatcher, one of the
greatest leaders of modern times
and Britain's finest prime minister
since Winston Churchill. Just before she was stabbed in the back
by traitors and turncoats, I was
invited to a reception with Mrs.
Thatcher at Stationers' Hall, the
magnificent London headquarters

Author Alan Franklin greets Lady Thatcher
during a campaign tour in June 2001.

of an ancient British livery company. There, in the shadow of St.
Paul's Cathedral, Mrs. Thatcher spoke forcefully without notes to a
small gathering of editors. She had a command of history, geography, economics, and science as well as politics and switched flu-
ently from one discipline to another. Both a trained barrister (top
lawyer) and research chemist, this lady has a magnificent mind
and, with President Reagan, her great friend, could share the credit
for ending the cold war. All who heard her that day were greatly
impressed. Who could challenge this woman, who could best her
in debate?

While the answer was "nobody," the plotting was by then well
underway in smoke-filled rooms in the Houses of Parliament, under Big Ben alongside the River Thames in London. The men who
brought her down didn't need to "best" her, they just needed to
hatch the plot which gave them the upper hand in any move against
her. My wife and I, by then aware of the double-dealing that
characterises the building of the European superstate, and the dark
forces behind it, knew she hadn't long left in power when she began to speak out strongly against the spreading of EU powers.

After one powerful speech in favour of drawing a line in the sand and ceding no more sovereignty to Brussels, I remember thinking: "You are not going to last long." Within weeks she was gone, in a tearful farewell to Downing Street, where she had ruled for eleven years. Under her leadership Britain was taken seriously in world councils and countries like Argentina, which foolishly invaded the Falkland Islands while she was prime minister. The Argentines learned that not for nothing was Mrs. Thatcher known as "The Iron Lady" when they found their massive invasion force having to surrender to British troops which stormed ashore to reclaim this British possession.

With Maggie gone, the way was clear for Britain to go full speed ahead into Europe. Her replacement, John Major, was a rather uninspiring leader, looking very much like the former bank clerk he once was. I met him at a Downing Street party just a few days after he had taken office. He wandered though from Number Ten (the prime minister's residence) to Number Eleven (residence of the chancellor of the exchequer), which are linked by an internal door. Nobody recognised him at first, and he started chatting to me, as I was the only one who noticed him. While pleasant

Former prime minister John Major greets Alan Franklin at a London reception in 1997. He presented Alan and Pat Franklin with a crystal bowl in recognition of their assistance to the Small Business Bureau and the Conservative Party, for whom Alan wrote the General Election public relations handbook.

enough, with no airs and graces, it was obvious that this was no leader in the Thatcher mould. With Maggie, you were in awe and proud to have met her. Even since her retirement she has been a major draw, speaking to tens of thousands of people at conferences round the world. Mr. Major, by contrast, was shy and diffident and, while being polite and pleasant if you wanted him to pose for a picture, did not inspire great confidence as a leader of the free world.

It is ironic that a former chief policy advisor to Major, Lord Blackwell, who led the Number Ten policy unit in the last years of

the Major government, now says that Britain must leave the European Union if a fresh wave of Thatcher-style free-market reforms is
to be launched in Britain. Within the EU, a pallid Socialist consensus rules and nothing likely to scare the horses is ever proposed as
leaders fudge and prevaricate. Writing in the *Times* of December
28, 2000, Lord Blackwell says Britain could prosper outside the
EU, following the example of Switzerland and Mexico in negotiat-
ing good trading deals while avoiding the web of red tape and rules
that make doing business in Europe such a burden.

Lord Blackwell, chairman of the Centre for Policy Studies, a
right-wing think-tank, says Britain's schools and hospitals, which
are currently lamentably failing despite billions of extra pounds
being poured into their coffers, should be run by the private sector
as part of a new wave of free market reforms. On membership of
the EU, Lord Blackwell says we no longer have to accept that there
is no alternative. Current Tory (Conservative) policy is for Britain
to stay inside the EU, but to fight to make it a more flexible organisation. Conservatives have spoken out strongly against the planned
Euro army, however. Defence spokesman Iain Duncan Smith MP,
who subsequently became party leader, says Prime Minister Blair
has spun "a web of deceit" to cover up "his Euro army agenda."

Incidentally, at the time of writing, Turkey has put a temporary
spoke in the wheel of this army's creation, rightly objecting that it
would harm and weaken NATO, of which Turkey is an important
member. Turkey has applied to become an EU member, though, so
will doubtless be brought to heel.

As Christina Speight, editor of *Facts, Figures and Phantasies*,
an anti-EU newsletter, said in her May 2000 editorial: "Your chains
are forged—a Euro dictatorship is planned." She said that the
parliament's constitutional affairs committee's proposals "make it
clear that what we are seeing looming on our horizon is not just an
emerging eurostate, as we have long feared, but a full-bodied euro
dictatorship." Pointing to the legislation to suspend political parties the EU does not approve of, she added: "So, the Europol
stormtroopers will be sent in to close down party branches. Just
like in the '20s and '30s. And who is to judge if a new party can be

suspended . . . why the existing parties of course." Yes, the coming Eurocorp—or should it be korps—may well one day be sent in to quell anti-EU protests on the streets of London or Edinburgh.

The European police state

This is how the *Daily Telegraph* of London depicted the fast-growing Euro police force—Europol.

Even Ireland is coming to realise that there are drawbacks to the truckloads of money flooding into its economy from Euro grants. They who pay the piper call the tune, and there are no free lunches, except for Brussels eurocrats. The Irish culture minister has said that the waves of Brussels directives and regulations are starting to "seriously impinge on our identity, culture and traditions." I don't see the freewheeling Irish taking too kindly to being ruled from Brussels, especially when their economy goes wrong and they are powerless to change economic policy. Countries like Ireland, Denmark, and Britain believe their freedoms are a right. On the rest of the continent the tendency is to think of them as favors granted by the state. Remember, most of Continental Europe does not have a long tradition of democracy.

It was on January 2, 1973, that Britain fulfilled its first EEC duties, for then the EU was called by the less alarming title "European Economic Union." Britain, Denmark, and Ireland sent representatives to Brussels to record their governments' assent to the first decisions taken by the newly enlarged community. These included confirmation of the appointment of members to the European Court of Justice in The Hague, Holland, and to the European Commission in Brussels. Against a background of flags on the fifteenth floor of the glass and marble building, handshakes were exchanged and a toast in champagne was drunk. Rather ominously, Britain's flag, the Union Jack, was flying upside down outside the building, where flags of the nine countries which were then members were on display. It was a low-key affair, Brussels being virtually deserted at the time because of the New Year holiday. Next day, the eurocrats tried again to fly Britain's flag. They again flew it upside down . . . Now, nearly thirty years on, the foul blue flag of Europe appears all over Britain, with the stars of the Madonna on everything from building plaques to car licence plates.

When I made a series of radio programmes with Dr. David Reagan of Lamb and Lion Ministries in Dallas in the summer of 2000, he asked me to quickly sum up the situation. Desperate to rouse unaware Americans to the great peril facing the world from faraway Europe, I said that the world should now be on red alert, as the present times looked so dangerous. With apocalyptic events perhaps just months away, such is the speed with which events are shaping up that we would all do well to forget about our stock market gains, pension plans, and new house purchases. If my reading of the situation is right, you won't be getting any pension. In fact, UN plans to curb the world population may mean that some of the most outlandish themes of science fiction films, where people are exterminated on reaching thirty, may not be so farfetched. Obviously life goes on, and until the Lord comes back for us we have to be wise stewards of our money; my point is not to trust in money. It's time to lay up treasure in heaven.

Satan hates the human race, God's greatest creation, so do not be surprised to see a series of measures to reduce the world's current six billion population. My wife Pat, interviewing one bureaucrat whose job it was to see that UN policies are adhered to, says he came close to admitting that the population must be slashed—but then realised what he was saying and bit his tongue.

It is ironic that our daughter was largely unsupported when she spoke at her college's student union against the motion that there are too many people in the world. The opposite is true—we need a lot more people! We are supposed to *fill* the earth, which we have not done, and we have been so brainwashed on the subject of population that anyone taking this stance will be laughed to scorn. Within weeks of the college population debate, news came out of Germany that leading politicians were worried that their population of around eighty-one million was aging fast, there would not be enough young people to look after the old and pay taxes, and that massive payments might have to be paid to mothers for each of their children for the first three years of their lives, to boost the birthrate.

At one school our daughter attended, a teacher gave them a weekend assignment—to come up with ideas on how to reduce the population of the earth. Ask your children if they have ever covered this as a topic at their school, possibly in a geography class. If they have, make a major fuss over it. Write not only to the school, but send copies to the school board, the local newspapers, radio and TV stations, state and national senators and representatives, and the state department of education. Go on the offensive and get this stinking thinking squelched! You will find a lot of people will support you and you will alert many who are still in blissful ignorance of the dangerous trends in our society.

But Christians must not worry. Jesus told us that God had provided information about the future. "The Spirit of truth . . . will shew you things to come. He shall glorify me: for he shall receive of mine, and shall shew it unto you" (John 16:13–14). The apostle Paul tells us that future events that will shake the world should not take us by surprise (1 Thess. 5:4). The population will be dramatically cut, perhaps by three-quarters, but this will be by the judgments poured out by God on a faithless, wicked people who would not turn to Him. First, as the Bible teaches, the true Christians will be taken out of the firing line—"in the twinkling of an eye."

Chapter 8

The Resurgent Spirit of Nazism

Which country is it which has brought bloodshed to all of Europe and beyond twice in a century? The country which has the biggest population in the European Union, an organisation which it dominates? Which country is it which is leading the charge to a unified Europe, which it will dominate? Germany is the one. Having failed to achieve world domination militarily and been left a smoking ruin in 1945, it has swiftly accomplished through peaceful means what its blitzkriegs never could. As the war becomes a distant memory, taught little in schools, and generations grow up even doubting that events like the Holocaust occurred, Germany is ever bolder in seeking the old, old prize. After the controversial summit in Nice, France, in December 2000, the headline in the *Times* of London was: "Germany triumphs on the E.U. battlefield," highlighting the fact that the Germans had secured for themselves the largest number of seats in the new, enlarged EU parliament—ninety-nine. Said the *Times:* "Germany emerged as the main victor in the marathon battle of Nice, winning more power and most of its other objectives in a new EU treaty." As German chancellor Gerhard Schroeder put it: "We must fulfill our historic duty: the idea of creating one single Europe." Already they are almost running Europe without a shot being fired . . .

An astonishing confirmation that the unification of Europe as an economic and political union was conceived by SS officers came in 2001, when public records were released from Britain's records office in Kew. These records, previously official secrets sealed for over fifty years, reveal that the Nazis even came up with the idea of a European army, a concept currently threatening to split Europe and America.

Major General Ellersiek and Brigadier Mueller, Hitler's chief of staff during the Battle of the Bulge, thought of the project as a way of keeping Nazism alive following what they realised would be an Allied victory in the Second World War. By March 1946, with Germany ruined, Ellersiek was in command of an underground political party called Organisation Suddeutschland which believed in setting up a fully armed, united Europe. He told a representative of British Intelligence, working under cover as a diplomat, that "what was important was that Britain should realise that if Europe was to survive we should all think 'as Europeans.'"

The former SS man said the party's manifesto called for "a pan-Europe as a balance between Russia and the USA." Although the nations would remain "independent," finance and defence matters would be decided centrally. "The good which was in Nazism still lives in the German heart," said Ellersiek. His party proposed "a new revolution for Germany which will set the pattern for Europe. . . . This revolution is to be the work of the new elite, the German prototype of the future rulers of Europe . . . which has emerged purified from Nazism and the trials of war."

The British intelligence man noted that German generals seemed likely to be in charge of this new Europe. "Germany must lead this New Europe with the cooperation of Britain," he revealed that Ellersiek had told him. He then added his own opinion that: "So little else of Britain is mentioned that it is evident that she is to be the junior partner." Jumping ahead to 2001, the new European army is headed by General Rainer Schuwirth of Germany, although Britain has provided much of the manpower and equipment. Prime Minister Tony Blair of Britain denies that what we have is a European army. Yet Romano Prodi, president of the European Commission, has openly admitted that "Europe is forging its own government and army." In the same statement he mocked the British leader's efforts to deny the truth, saying: "If you don't want to call it a European army, don't call it a European army. You can call it Margaret or Mary-Anne."

When our daughter Anne attended what was claimed to be, academically, the "top school in Hampshire," a position its examination results could justify, I sometimes chatted to her friends on the drive in. One day I was talking about World War Two. The girls had little idea of what had happened in grandad's day, perhaps even when their own parents had been alive. "Was that between England and Poland?" asked one. Well, it is true that the German invasion of Poland *had* set off the war, and this was what caused Britain to issue its ultimatum to the Nazis. But it was just a part of a huge mosaic about which these girls clearly had little concept.

Worse was to come. Osprey, the educational publishers, commissioned a study of British schoolchildren's historical knowledge—and concluded that it had hit a "shocking low." Not only was the First World War a mystery to two-thirds of secondary age schoolchildren, but some even thought Adolph Hitler was Britain's Second World War prime minister! Five percent of the eleven- to eighteen-year-olds surveyed thought the Roman occupation of Britain was a mere one hundred fifty years ago. This survey, published in January 2001, was of children allegedly taught history up to the age of fourteen, in the cases of those fourteen and older. I thought then: "Those who do not understand history are condemned to repeat its mistakes. . . ."

At the same time my wife and daughter attended three history lessons being taught at one of Britain's leading universities. They

How British newspapers told of the formation of a new European army, a French idea inspired by the prospect of cutting America out of the military and political picture and weakening NATO.

were being given a "sample" of what was on offer as my daughter was in the course of choosing her university. Lecturer one lauded the America of the corrupt Kennedys before rolling his eyes and saying, "and then, of course, along came Nixon and Reagan"—cue for his students to gasp in horror.

Next they looked in on a class taught by a woman historian showing a very silly film from the forties which had all the cliches of the age, but was at least modest and lacking in expletives. "Ms. Right-On" then spoke scathingly of film censorship. The conclusion the class was required to draw was: "how dreadfully stupid and repressive."

The last class was worst and left my wife and daughter shell-shocked. This was the scoffer teaching medieval history and showing pictures of Christians being boiled alive and having nails driven through their eyes. Before each grisly scene he primed his class with a jokey remark, so that when the awful scenes flashed up they laughed out loud, as the lecturer wanted.

This man found visions of hell particularly mirth making. Let's hope he enjoys it as much when he gets there. I tell these firsthand stories of my family's experiences to show how easy it is to program atheism, humanism, and Socialism into our students today. When believers really are being martyred again in the Great Tribulation, do not think these brainwashed young people will step in to help. They will probably gather round for the spectacle, as crowds did in Imperial Rome when Nero used burning Christians to light his parties.

I now turn to an article in the *Daily Telegraph* of October 4, 2000, headed: "Germany is model for uniting Europe." The story was filed from Dresden, a city almost destroyed by firebombs in World War Two, and said that Germany's Chancellor Schroeder and France's President Chirac had vowed to use the modern Germany as a model for uniting the whole of Europe, as they celebrated ten years since unification of East and West Germany, when the Berlin Wall came down. Speaking in the eastern city of Dresden, they insisted that the rebuilding of Europe had only just begun, something which would have astonished the British and American troops whose efforts from 1945 onward got the shattered country on its feet again. It was the British Royal Engineers who set up the Volkswagen factory, having found a few working prototypes of Hitler's "people's car" and established a production line of the model that was to become the modern world's "Model T." The Anglo-Saxons of Britain and America are given little credit for their efforts, and the mountain of American Marshall Aid money, which got the Germans on their feet and off the food lines after their defeat.

Said Germany's Schroeder: "After overcoming the German division, overcoming the division of the continent is now the main task of Germany's foreign and security policy. Today we not only celebrate German unity but also the newly won prospect of a united Europe." Chirac agreed, calling on the German people to prepare themselves for EU enlargement and further integration with people beyond their borders. He added that those who had fought totalitarianism had "opened the way to the unification of all Europe." Hundreds of thousands of Germans celebrated the occasion and the plans for their greater influence over an enlarged EU. Germany will be the geographical, political, and economic heart of the expanded EU. After ten years of talking, the superpower is preparing to open membership to new entrants from the east. The present fifteen-member EU could double in numbers in four or five years, with countries like Poland, Hungary, Latvia, Malta, Cyprus, and Lithuania just itching to give up their sovereignty. They see only trade and export advantages and are seemingly oblivious to the loss of their independence that membership will bring.

Germany will be the fulcrum of the new, enlarged EU, as a glance at the map of Europe will confirm. Germany, already the most powerful and economically successful nation in the EU, currently lies on the EU's eastern boundary, with the vast pool of cheap Eastern European labor on its doorstep. Once the great surge east has taken place, from 2004 onward, Berlin will be the centre of the new empire, just as Adolph Hitler planned sixty years earlier. He always told his people that they had to look east for enlargement and already a wave of German money has swept eastward, with huge amounts invested in the former Soviet Empire, including Russia itself. Poland is now a prime target of German investment and source of cheap labor. As its influence follows its money, Germany has lately been playing a different, more dominant role in Europe. The war-guilt has gone and Germany is no longer content to let France take the lead, as was illustrated at the Nice summit.

In a story datelined December 4, 2000, the *Times* reported: "Schroeder rejects parity with France." The report said that Germany refused to give ground to France on key demands for European reform and added that Chancellor Schroeder rejected President Chirac's pleas for equal status between France and Germany. Germany, with eighty-two million inhabitants, roughly twenty million more than France, Italy, and Great Britain, thinks it is time that this population imbalance was reflected in more votes for itself in the EU. Germany's Schroeder told reporters: "I cannot accept a weighting of votes that will give Spain, or later Poland, as many votes as Germany, which has double the number of citizens. That is not acceptable; everything will unravel." The chemistry is clearly changing in the EU, which was once promoted by the French as a means of controlling Germany after the last war.

France always believed that if it tied itself closely to its aggressive neighbour it would never again be attacked. The original six countries that were the core of what became the EU had this as objective number one: controlling German militarism in the future. It now seems clearer that a new German empire is being created by stealth, not war. "First among equals" was how the *Times* saw Germany's new role in the enlarged EU after the Nice summit. As well as winning more MEPs than France, Britain, or Italy, the three other "big" countries of the EU, Germany also succeeded in getting another summit meeting of the organisation in 2004, at which time many feel the final integration of the continent into one country will be accomplished.

Many newspapers throughout Europe concluded after Nice that German power had been increased. She became the only country able to block a decision by joining with two other big countries, on the basis of a double majority system based on population. Accord-

ing to German newspaper *Die Welt* (December 12, 2000): "The direction of European policy for the coming years will be based on
two ideas which were originally very German." These two key ideas,
agreed at Nice, are to draw up a European constitution by 2004
and to have a hard-core of "fast forward" states clustered around
Germany, an area of "enhanced cooperation." This cuts out the
chances of awkward Nordic or British people throwing spanners
in the works.

Said the *Times* in a report on December 12, 2000: "The Ger-
man-inspired plan for 2004 is already being depicted as the likely
vehicle for a European constitution, a prospect that will cause severe pain for the British political world. It will determine the status of the Charter of Fundamental Rights which Britain has pledged
to prevent ever becoming legally binding." It seems the Germans
may also chair the next EU summit, to ensure they get their way in
shaping the new Europe in the Germanic mould. The problem is
that in a new union of twenty-seven or twenty-eight members, how
will any contentious measure get unanimous backing? This is why
it is essential for countries to be stripped of their vetoes over important areas of policy. Britain gave up approximately thirty-nine
veto options at Nice, allowing majority voting to prevail in everything from anti-discrimination measures, with their potential for
big problems for Christian churches, to measures for introducing
the European currency. It held on to its veto in a handful of things
like tax and social security matters. Tax is lighter in Britain than in
Germany, something the Germans are keen to change, to the benefit of their industry.

The very bureaucratic unwieldiness currently built into the
creaking EU rulebook is bound to cause increasing frustration
among member states. After five days of chaotic wrangling in Nice,
even Prime Minister Blair said: "We can't go on like this." One
move that surprised observers came when Blair gave up the veto
over the European president. If dark days return to Europe, economic decay will mean that the cumbersome decision making process *has* to be reformed into something much more streamlined.
This is the time when I envisage the "man of action" Europe is

waiting for to step out from the shadows. He will offer inspired leadership and may even make the trains run on time. Troublesome elements will be roughly put in their place and a new, firm hand will be detected behind law and order policies. Mr. Blair may live to realise that giving up that veto was the most unwise step he ever took . . .

Democratic rights are unlikely to feature largely in the new German-dominated Europe. Writing in the anti-EU newsletter *Facts, Figures and Phantasies* of January 2001, editor Christina Speight commented:

> [British prime minister] Blair comes back from Nice talking of the two vetoes he has kept. He keeps very quiet about the 30 or more that he has surrendered. . . . The best he can crow about is that he has only given up our sole right in 30 or more areas. These include the regulation of political parties, border controls, visas, asylum, refugees, illegal immigrations, financial aid to other members, external representation on international bodies, trade and commercial policy, trade union law, industry, co-operation with other countries, overseas territories, MEPs, rules for the European Court of Justice as well as a number of important but procedural questions. In all these areas we are all now less independent than we were, but Blair claims credit for keeping the veto in two areas!"

The feisty editor adds:

> Dealing with the EU is similar to being embraced by an octopus. Until Nice we were embraced by the beast with five tentacles and were slowly suffocating as a country. At Nice another two tentacles tried to wrap themselves around us and Blair stopped one. So now we are in the grip of six—some achievement for him to be proud of! This treaty is—as predicted—an utter disaster for Britain and is one more step in the building of the EU superstate. And that is just the treaty. There was also the Charter of Rights, which all except Blair realise is the embryonic constitution of the

EU superstate (and all politicians on the continent say so). This has now been adopted and the European Court will 'take it into account' when deciding on judgements.

Then there's the Euro-Army (or not the European army as the British government pretends.) This German-led army, incidentally, was stated by German foreign minister Joschka Fischer to be "another pillar in the process of European unification." Some leaders like Blair fondly imagine they will continue to have a veto on the use of their troops in this new army. However, there has never been a veto which the EU did not try to abolish or weaken. Lady Thatcher has seen through it, describing it as "a piece of monumental folly that puts our security at risk in order to satisfy political vanity."

The trouble with the EU is that no step is ever final: each demands a follow-up, to a final, nightmarish dictatorship, the rules of which are now nearly all in place, ready for the final dictator. It is the German Mr. Fischer who tells it like it is, calling the euro "a quantum leap" toward federalism, creating a "federal bank" that imposes an inexorable "federal logic" on all the participants. Now the French want a single economic authority to put steel into the euro. This will make national economic decision-taking ever more irrelevant. The Germans only agreed to the euro because they thought it would really be a "euro-deutschsmark," with them in charge. I predict they soon will be.

The old Germany, with its lust for dominance and racial intolerance, has by no means been buried, as was shown in a firebomb attack on a synagogue in the West German town of Dusseldorf. This brought these scary comments from Paul Spiegel, leader of Germany's Jewish community: "After such repeated attacks on synagogues . . . one is justifiably entitled to ask whether it was right to rebuild Jewish communities in Germany. What more needs to happen before Germans grasp the hatred that is on the loose in their country?" There are also ominous signs from the former East Germany, where far-right groups are gaining strength as the economy stagnates. The French news agency AFP reported in March 2001 that the granddaughter of the assassinated Israeli prime minister,

Yitzhak Rabin, said that she was barred from a Munich restaurant. Noa Ben Artzi-Pelossof said the restaurateur said he wanted to have "nothing to do with Jews."

Recent research has shown that wartime Germans were perfectly happy to have Jews and many other groups eliminated and that groups such as doctors went along with sterilisation and selective breeding programs to eliminate genetic imperfection. A TV program called "Science and the Swastica: Hitler's biological soldiers," screened on Britain's Channel Four in March 2001, showed that ordinary Germans knew and colluded with Nazi ideas. Doctors were the number one profession among members of the SS and many of them relished stealing the jobs of their former Jewish colleagues. Hitler said that doctors were "more important to the Nazi regime than almost any other." They were willing to kill sick and disabled babies to achieve the perfect race, eliminating lives "unworthy of life." Just as today's abortionists do, using weasel words to avoid telling the stark truth of the holocaust of the unborn. Those now pressing for legal euthanasia should remember that the first gas chambers in Germany were built to murder almost one hundred thousand disabled people and psychiatric patients.

A Berlin-based polling organisation produced a startling result when it asked Germans aged fourteen to twenty-five about the Nazis. It seems lots of them would welcome the Fascists back into power! Half the German young people said they thought Hitler and his henchmen had "good points" and nearly one in six said the Nazi Party itself was "a good idea." This helps explain why 13,753 xenophobic and anti-Semitic crimes occurred in 2000, up from 9,456 in 1999. Physical attacks against foreigners went up from 397 to 553—around thirty percent. Around half the violent attacks were in East Germany. Unemployment and a moral vacuum following Communism's collapse are blamed by some observers.

Political scientist Helmut Griese of the University of Frankfurt said: "We all take democracy for granted in Germany, but it is a fragile democracy, one that has been in existence for just fifty years. And the ghosts of the street battles between Communists and Nazis are rattling their chains in the collective conscience all the time. That our youth still believes the perpetrators of the biggest mass slaughter in history had 'good points' boggles the mind." The leader of Germany's parliament, Wolfgang Thierse, has painted an apocalyptic picture of a country (the former East Germany) on the verge of collapse and without hope, despite the fact that Western nations have so far pumped over $300 billion into the former workers' paradise. In a leaked secret report Mr. Thierse, president of the Bundestag, the German parliament, says billions more dollars are needed to avoid the total collapse of the eastern half of Germany.

"The economic and social situation of eastern Germany is balanced precariously on the brink," he wrote in the report to leaders of the eastern states. "Stagnation in gross national product, productivity, income and jobs has created a grave situation." He goes on to describe a society of hatred, despair, poverty, crime, and joblessness with silent steel furnaces, disused coalfields, and decrepit docks along the Baltic coastline. There are one hundred fifty thousand young people on the dole, most of them under twenty-five, while forty-six percent of all Germany's right-wing hate crimes are committed in East Germany, which has just a fifth of the country's eighty-two million people. Warns Mr. Thierse: "The East will continue to be a breeding ground for the far right until solutions are found." "Solutions" are unlikely, as economists reckon the East needs another $450 billion, money which is unlikely to appear as it can be invested more profitably in places like China.

It is clear that all the Eastern European countries which were misruled by Communists for so long need massive investment. Without it, some of them at least will become real trouble-grounds. Remember, it takes serious economic problems for dictators to come to power. "History's great inflations have almost always been followed by a dictator who promised among other things to restore the currency's value. Napoleon, Hitler and Mao Tse-tung all rode to power on the back of hyper-inflation" (*Time*, March 10, 1980). Hitler came in after citizens had been carrying their wages home in wheelbarrows! As nations in Europe reflect on the need for a strong man to sort out their problems, Europe has been demanding yet more powers for Brussels in order to avoid policy drift. From a ghostly Berlin bunker a clap of approval may perhaps have been heard . . .

Adolf Hitler, the last man who tried to unite Europe under one government with one currency.

Adolph Hitler was a man who believed in arresting policy drift and taking strong and decisive action. He also pursued the goal of a united Europe and was enthusiastically in favour of expanding its borders. He was, in fact, the perfect modern European, a forerunner of Antichrist. One well-known preacher I know told me he thought Antichrist would be a resurrected Hitler! Many of Hitler's principles have uncanny modern echoes. He banned hunting on horseback, just as today's animal rights protestors would do. His ban on hunting with dogs is in force even today in Germany. Teetotaler and vegetarian, his first dictatorial act was to ban the cooking of lobsters, as he found their screams distressing when they were thrown into boiling water. The screams of people did not bother him.

Like "Friends of the Earth" and "Greenpeace" today, the Nazis had a strong sentimentality about "nature." I am not equating these organisations with Nazis, but they do share a moral righteousness which sometimes justifies law breaking, like occupying buildings and oil rigs. Greenies in general also have a tendency to regard "people" as the main problem for "Mother Earth." I often see this in their alarmingly hostile letters to me at the newspaper, which regularly screech that there are "too many people," and in comments made to me by green enthusiasts I know well. The Nazis agreed and caused over sixty million people to be "culled" in the Second World War, either in battles or extermination camps.

The Nazis regarded those opposed to them as beneath contempt, while today in Britain masked and club wielding "animal rights" demonstrators regard their cause as so righteous that it gives them the "right" to attack and club those they disagree with. Similarly,

militant "animal rights" supporters have car-bombed cars belong-
ing to workers in laboratories where research on animals is carried out, or supporters of hunts. The managing director of a research laboratory was attacked outside his home in Britain in 2001
by baseball-bat wielding terrorists
acting in the name of "animals."
Similarly, the Jews were seen as
"anti-natural" by Hitler's chief mur-
derer, Heinrich Himmler, who regarded shooting birds or animals as
"pure murder" and was proud of
how the ancient Germanic peoples
had respect for animals. Today some
farms which grow crops opposed by
Greenpeace have their property destroyed. They are "anti-nature," after all, so that's all right then.

Uncle Sam rides
out to fight for
British rights

This American delegation is marching in
support of another British freedom soon to be
lost—the right to hunt on horseback.

   Shops which sold furs were firebombed, so furs are rarely
openly marketed today, and even butchers' shops have been attacked and damaged in the name of the "rights" of animals. Fisher-
men on lonely riverbanks have been attacked by vegetarian animal
rights fanatics in a campaign set to escalate. In wartime Germany,
Himmler, an enthusiast of Buddhism as so many are today, even
considered fitting his SS thugs with bells to stop them treading on
small creatures at night. He wrote an article called "animal rights"
for the SS magazine in 1934 in which he praised medieval Germans for putting rats on trial and giving them the chance to change
their ways.

   Hitler would also have gone down the modern road of opposition to shooting and fishing, which is far more advanced today in
Britain, for example, than it yet is in America. Goering was another politically correct Nazi, who in a 1933 radio broadcast said
he had stopped vivisection in Prussia. German scientists later conducted their worst experiments on the children of slave workers
and prisoners, but Hitler's number two said that anyone flouting
animal rights would be thrown into jail. Hitler even tried a meat-

free diet for his alsation dog—the one he loved so much that he tested his cyanide on her before he poisoned himself in his bunker. Hitler's fanatical anti-smoking stance may also strike a few modern chords. As he was losing the war in March 1944, he found time to ban smoking on tramcars lest it affect the conductors' health. You were allowed to plan mass murder in Nazi Party offices—but woe betide you if you smoked!

Hitler's strange priorities

This article showed how up to date Hitler's thinking is. He was a vegetarian, New Age thinker, deep into the occult, and a keen "animal liberationist." He also tried to ban smoking!

Like the New Agers, Hitler's beliefs were rooted in the occult. When he was working as an artist in Vienna as a young man, he spent much of his spare time in occult bookstores, becoming obsessed with mind expansion, transcendental meditation, astrology, yoga and so-called "white" and "black" magic. Like many earth and witchcraft obsessed young people today, he speeded up the mind-expansion by drug taking, opening up his mind to full demonic possession, something which became evident much later in his—literally—spellbinding speeches, scripted by Satan himself. Hitler used mescaline to "open up his mind" and was convinced he had communicated with Lucifer himself. Hermann Rauschning, president of the Nazis' senate in Danzig, reported that his master had terrible, fearful nights, when he was stalked by a hideous phantom that seemed very real to the Führer.

Rauschning said Hitler often used to wake up screaming and described how he sat on the edge of his bed, gasping for breath and screaming out: "It's him, it's him, he's here." He then counted some numbers aloud, muttered some meaningless phrases, and then yelled: "There, over there, in the corner. Who is it?"—by which time he was howling and jumping up and down. Hitler was bad, not mad; he was demon possessed, not insane. I have no way of confirming it, but it is possible that he was possessed by the spirit of Satan himself, the ultimate hater of Jews and Christians. So it is easy to see where his searing hatred of the Jews originated. Through

their rallies, symbolism, initiation ceremonies, absurd quests for
the "Holy Grail," whatever they thought that was, occultism per-
meated the Nazi beliefs. The two were one and the same.

Nazis and the coalition of greens and the spiritually misguided
who form today's New Age movement have similar esoteric roots
and paganism at their core. Like New Agers, the Nazis adopted the
summer solstice as an important ritual and Hitler stated: "The old
pagan beliefs will be brought back to honor again . . . the whole
secret knowledge of nature, of the divine, the demonic." The Nazis
and New Agers share the doctrine of Aryanism which reaches back
into the mists of Atlantean fables to show that Aryans were the
leading race of the seven which allegedly inhabited Atlantis. They
believe they have more highly developed intellects and both have
initiates, adepts, and masters, with those at the top sharing little of
their inner knowledge or psycho/spiritual power. Nazis delighted
in pastoral idylls with flaxen haired girls gaily haymaking in the
fields; New Age greenies echo this love of Mother Nature, worship
earth goddess Gaia, and hark back to a mythical past when nature
spirits and men allegedly communed freely. "May Gaia be with you"
is a greeting I spotted on the bottom of one of their newsletters.

Jesus said that as it was in the days of Noah, so will it be in the
days of the coming of the Son of Man—in other words, at his return. Dark demonic forces were highly active in the days of Noah,
just as they are today. The world of Noah's time had to be destroyed,
apart from Noah and his immediate family, as Genesis 6 tells. The
world today is also on the verge of destruction by God, along with
a large part of its inhabitants. The reasons are the same: idol worship and evil rather than, as the Nazis believed, the "wrong" bloodline. In truth the Jews had the right bloodline and the fact that they
have kept it intact for two thousand years of dispersion is a miracle
as great as the parting of the Red Sea. Satan is still interested in a
"final solution" for them because this is the only way he thinks he
has a chance of thwarting God's plan to save mankind.

Alice Bailey, "mother" of the New Age movement, wrote dis-
paragingly of the Jews in her book *Esoteric Healing* in which she
said they had an "evil karma" and "parasitic" tendencies. In *The*

Hidden Dangers of the Rainbow, a bestselling book authored in 1983 by Christian lawyer Constance Cumbey, Mrs.Cumbey points out: "The Nazi theme of Aryan purity is found throughout the Alice Bailey books." My view is that Satan doesn't change his plot. Looking at the amazing similarities in New Ageism and Nazism, amply documented in Mrs. Cumbey's book, I am almost tempted to join them in their belief in reincarnation(!).

France's interior minister, Jean Pierre Chevenment, says that Germany has not recovered from Nazism. He stated in May 2000: "At the bottom of this, Germany is still dreaming of the German Holy Roman Empire. It has not yet healed from the historical accident of Nazism." Mr. Chevenment does not know it, but the reason is that there is a spiritual dimension to all this: the same spirit behind Nazism is now behind the New Age, one-world, one-faith movement that is currently pushing Europe together into one sinister, satanic superstate. This superstate will be ruled from Germany and, according to one Christian in a position to have seen the politics of the situation unfold at close quarters, it will be ruled by a satanic entity that holds sway over Bavaria—seat and foundation stone of the Nazi Party and of German militarism.

All leading Nazis were occultists. Their very symbols and ceremonies screamed "occult" and their slogan "blood and fire" is lifted straight from witchcraft. SS leader Himmler was so obsessed with the occult that he looted one hundred forty thousand books on witchcraft from libraries across Europe and set up a unit to investigate and publicise the issue. A Poznan librarian found the witchcraft library in a palace in Lower Silesia and found that books had been marked in places where tortures were described. Himmler not only ran the SS, the Waffen SS, and the Gestapo, and supervised the concentration camps, he ran the Lebensborn project aimed at creating a Nordic super race.

This has odd echoes in today's projects to clone perfect human beings and the constant striving for the "perfect body" urged on us all by numerous magazines and TV shows. Hitler's New Reich Church had a very modern-seeming ecumenical slogan: "One people, one reich, one faith," as long as it wasn't faith in biblical

Christianity, of course. Hitler, who adopted the Hindu occult symbol of the swastica as his own, was a strong proponent of the so-called ancient wisdom, or Hinduism, which today holds sway in the West. So which "wise person" sent Hitler as a gift to the world, I wonder? Hitler and his cohorts were forerunners, types of the terror which is to come. It will be far bigger and deadlier than Nazism, with the full array of modern electronics to use to control its terrified subjects, who will wear its leader's mark on their right hands or foreheads—or be killed.

Nothing changes, as Satan has no new tricks. The rebirth of Germany and its move to centre stage in Europe is a striking feature of the past few years as the old, apologetic Germany has vanished. Berlin, with its rebuilt Reichstag, is again the powerhouse at the crossroads of Europe, a place to which American presidents travel, seeking favor. In Berlin, setting for the decadence depicted in the musical *Cabaret*, hundreds of cranes are busily rebuilding the city to which the parliament has now returned. The successors to Bismark, who tried to unite Europe under the Prussians in the nineteenth century, want to bury Germany's past—while at the same time setting about their old, domination agenda. There is something symbolic about Germany moving its post-war capital from sleepy, rural Bonn to powerhouse Berlin, being revitalised by huge projects, like the building of the biggest railway station in Europe, vast government complexes, and the emergence of a new German political class determined to seize their destiny once more. Germany would never have agreed to abandon the deutschmark had it not believed it could control the new euro, launched as it was from Frankfurt.

The year 2001 also saw a celebration of a revived Prussia—a state dissolved fifty-three years ago by the victorious Allies for being "militaristic and reactionary" and forcefully backing Hitler. "Prussian Year 2001 was backed by the governments of Berlin and the next-door state of Brandenburg to celebrate the three hundredth anniversary of the coronation of Frederick I in 1701, the first Prussian king. Over one hundred museums and cultural centres held Prussian-centered events and celebrations in a bid to give the

Prussians a new image. Berlin officials said that Prussian Year
would not focus unduly on the state's historic urge to march into
its neighbors' lands, but would look at "Prussian modesty, state
service, discipline and thrift." Brandenburg is in fact a state infamous for neo-Nazi attacks on foreigners and anti-Semitism, but its
officials said that Prussian Year should focus in strengthening pride
in "one's own country."

Prussian and Nazi power were two branches of the same tree,
and Professor Wolfgang Wipperman of Berlin's Free University
sounds a watchman's warning when he says: "It is all very well to
emphasise the positive aspects of Prussia, such as its religious tolerance and legal system, but the state was anything but a parliamentary democracy. *There is currently a strange nostalgia for this
non-democratic form of state.*"

The German industries which for years fought against paying
compensation to millions of slave workers, in companies like
Mercedes and Volkswagen, now see little to apologise for as once
again they set out on foreign takeovers. Seven million non-Jewish
slave workers joined two million Jews in making Hitler's war machine work, under Albert Speer's direction. Yet only in recent times
has there been any move toward compensation, and this strictly
for reasons of business rather than humanity. These enormous
German concerns, firms like Siemens and Deutsche Bank, even
hired historians to gloss up their past, omitting all the awkward
bits about looting and slavery. The corporate history of Volkswagen
described the wartime slave laborers as "foreign labor" living in "a
multicultural society."

In a British war crimes trial, the story was told of how four
hundred babies born to women slaves at Volkswagen's vast
Wolfsberg plant were taken from them and killed. The VW story is
that these babies were victims of an epidemic in a nursery. Yet the
doctor involved was executed for mass murder. Volkswagen's directors accepted this sanitised "history." Among them was Gerhard
Schroeder, Germany's current leader. Unembarrassed about its past,
Daimler Benz has taken over Chrysler of the USA, having tricked
the Americans into thinking this was some kind of merger of equals,

which was how it was sold to shareholders. By late 2000 the last of the senior American management had departed the Chrysler plants, which were firmly in the hands of the men from the firm of the five-pointed star. Condescendingly, they said that American management might be reappointed after several years of reorganisation.

A new study of the Nazis, *The Third Reich: A New History*, by Michael Burleigh, argues that Nazism was a religion. He tells how this National Socialism, with its theology, liturgy, and symbolism, aimed to create Hitler's "new man," ruthless in order to fulfill his Darwinian destiny. In recruiting men to the SS, Himmler was as hostile to atheists as he was to Christians. The whole truth, obvious to anyone with a background in the occult, can be seen by watching many of the heavily pagan Nazi propaganda films, which are very "Mother Earth" orientated. The themes of blood, folk, fire, and soil—the very constituents of paganism and witchcraft—are becoming just as popular today as they were at the time of Hitler's rise to power in the 1930s. I must reiterate that there was no political movement "greener" than National Socialism. In order to "save the earth" we may just have to sacrifice a few million people—or a few thousand million! Few are as fervent as the evangelisers of environmentalism. Fired with the moral righteousness of old-time preachers, they condemn the sinners who use oil, gas, consume goods, and generally "spoil" the earth.

Go into any classroom in any western country and I can guarantee that "saving the earth" from wicked mankind is a theme. Sinful men are about to cut down the last tree. Forests are going, food is becoming scarce, we are running out of everything. In fact, while it is true that we should look after God's creation, as He would wish us to, most environmentalism is unwarranted alarmism. The world is *not* running out of oil, for example. Most of the world has yet to be explored for oil-bearing rocks, and there are believed to be countless billions of barrels of crude beneath seabeds in places like the Falkland Islands, or under the wilderness of Alaska. It is even more important now to develop it, to lessen our dependence on unreliable Islamic countries who may well not be our "allies" for long.

I used to believe all the claptrap about "only 30 years supply of oil in the world" and, in 1974, wrote a series of articles for a newspaper in America, wisely telling readers that they would have to give up their cars as we would all soon be back to walking. Such is a young man's wisdom. Then I bought a book called *The Energy Non-Crisis* by a man named Lindsay Williams. Lindsay was chaplain to the builders of the Trans-Alaska oil pipeline and wrote his book in 1980 after being astounded at the amount of oil being discovered in Alaska—and then being sealed up again! This is an extract: "After only one week on the north slope of Alaska, Senator Chance had said to me, 'Almost everything said to me [about the energy crisis] by those briefers from Washington, D.C., was a lie.'"

Then again:

> After proving the find at Gull Island an ARCO executive went on to say, 'Chaplain, America has just become energy independent!' . . . The energy crisis had just come to a screeching halt—this ought to hit the front page of every newspaper in America . . . but before an announcement was made, the government forced them to cap it and seal the records which documented the find . . . WHY?!?' At that point I decided it was time for somebody to tell this story . . . of a scandal greater than Watergate!

At the time he wrote his book (with Dr. Clifford Wilson), Lindsay Williams had been a Baptist minister for twenty-eight years and went to Alaska in 1971 as a missionary. After becoming chaplain to the pipeline workers, he was given executive status with the Alyeska Pipeline Company which gave him access to the information published in his book, which is one every American should read.

Ex-senator Hugh M. Chance from Colorado went to the pipeline to see for himself what was going on. He was told by an oil company executive:

> If we as oil companies were allowed to develop the entire North Slope oil field, that is the entire area north of the Brooks Range in Alaska, producing the oil that we already know is there, and if

we were allowed to tap the numerous pools of oil that could be tapped (we are tapping only one right now), in five years the United States could be . . . totally independent from the rest of the world as far as energy is concerned. What is more, sir, if we were allowed to develop this entire field as private enterprise, within five years the United States of America could balance payments with every nation on the face of the earth, and again be the great nation America really should be. We could do that if only private enterprise was allowed to operate freely, without government intervention.

Private enterprise, if it were ever allowed to get on with the job, could solve "energy non-problems" as the quotes from this book show. If fuel ever becomes scarce, the price goes up. This gives the incentive to find resources in more difficult areas. It is far from a pressing problem, yet is being used as an excuse to control people, particularly in Britain where what I call "the big green lie machine" has given the government the excuse to raise the price of gasoline to around six dollars a gallon. If you prevent people from driving where they want to, you are taking away the fundamental freedom of movement and association. You also make people housebound—housebound by price pressures—and therefore easier to control. Of course, one-world government enthusiasts do not want any country, especially mighty America, to be "energy self-sufficient." They want mutual reliance, interdependence and, most of all, Socialist state control of the whole world.

The green Nazi agenda of today is every bit as effective as National Socialist Goebbels' lies for Hitler and his henchmen. If you repeat that the earth faces global warming often enough on nightly TV news, most people believe it. If you constantly tell children the earth is running out of trees, they believe you, notwithstanding that Canada and America, to name but two, are virtually wall to wall trees. You can drive for days through, for example, New England, and see nothing but millions and millions of trees, all carefully tended and cropped so they go on paying dividends.

In Britain, the first thing most householders do when they move into a new home is to plant trees. Yet these are the people who have been conned that there are almost no trees left! In the area where my paper circulates, you can be prosecuted for trimming a branch off what Americans would regard as a weed tree. I met someone who chopped down a straggly sycamore tree which had grown up through a disused coal bunker. For this he was taken to criminal court and fined! If you dare to point out the illogicality and stupidity of any of this, the greenies' wrath is upon your head. Because I supported the retention of an airfield in our district, a group of enviroloonies marched through the town waving banners saying: "Alan Franklin is an enemy of the people." Of these people, certainly . . .

You see, what I had challenged was not a viewpoint, it was a faith. A faith just like Nazism. Most greens are innocent of all this. They just haven't thought through their political antecedents. However, it is true that greens are absolutists and more vehement than many religious fundamentalists. They believe we are afloat on a godless Spaceship Earth, and unless drastic action is taken earth is at risk. Do not be surprised if this drastic action includes the culling of inconvenient people, especially the elderly who need expensive hospital treatment or nursing home care. If people are constantly portrayed as the problem, as the blot on the face of "Mother," as they are in our schools, it follows that the removal of large numbers of people will solve earth's problems. Hence a recent surge in support for euthanasia—a straw in the wind, I can assure you.

In November 2000 euthanasia was finally legalised in Holland, one of Europe's most permissive and liberal countries. In practice, "mercy killing" has been a feature of Dutch life for years, but although a blind eye was turned to it, it was not legal until now. In 1999 Dutch euthanasia organisations said that 2,216 patients were "helped" to die by their doctors. The new law says that adult patients must have made a voluntary and well thought through request to die and they must also face "unremitting and unbearable suffering" if they were to carry on living. Those asking to die must be briefed by a doctor and be fully aware of their medical situation. This echoes the tight restrictions that were first placed on abortions, in both America and Britain. Once the principle was established the liberal lobby soon made sure the strings were loosened and today we have virtual abortion on demand. A similar pattern can be expected with euthanasia. The more of God's special creation that is destroyed, the more Satan loves it. This is yet another consequence of most people not knowing, and of young people not being taught, basic Bible truths.

It is superficially odd that greenies, who believe themselves to be liberal, are in fact very hard line and will brook no dissent. Try and build a road and they damage your vehicles. At a road improvement project a mile from my Hampshire home, green extremists had the effrontery to daub the words "eco vandals" on the machinery, evidently not seeing the irony in their actions. They are the world's fastest growing political movement, with a young base which will grow in importance as these people move into adult society. I have no doubt that they will form part of the base of the future Antichrist's power system—his storm troopers, perhaps. They already practice on huntsmen and farmers, after all, using firebombs, knives, clubs, and stones in Britain to try and stop foxhunting. Because Communism is now a dead philosophy, his base will also include the real hard right, who are growing in importance and electoral strength throughout Europe.

A curious thing happened in the summer of 2000. South Africa was about to be awarded the football (soccer) world cup, in 2006. Everyone in FIFA, football's governing body, appeared to think this was the right place. Africa was overdue such an honor and South Africa is undoubtedly the best run country on the continent. Suddenly, from nowhere, Germany rose and grabbed the prize. Dirty tricks were suspected. New Zealand's representative fled the country, saying he had been put under dreadful pressure in casting his vote. So Deutschland triumphed and, to show that it really doesn't care too much what the world thinks, has chosen to hold the opening and closing matches of these games, televised into the majority of the world's homes—in Hitler's 1936 Olympic Stadium.

This venue of the infamous Nazi games, when the whole show and its theatrical symbolism was used to glorify Hitler and the Nazis,

is to be expensively restored for the occasion. Berlin is now raising
£180 million to restore the stadium that Hitler had built as a setting for the triumph of the Aryan race. Hitler's Olympic Village has
stood since those terrifying days, largely unused. Work on restor-
ing it started on the day the Germans won the vote in Zurich, a fact
which in itself is suspicious. How is it that they were so ready, with
builders waiting, one wonders? The stadium in its new/old incar-
nation will seat seventy-six thousand and will have a VIP guest
area. The stadium is a protected monument, so the restoration ar-
chitects can do little to remove traces of its Nazi past. When the
football matches take place in 2006, I wonder if a new dictator will
be taking his place on the podium?

Chapter 9

A Parliament for the New World Order

Can you imagine a world parliament, a latter day Babel after God intervened to confuse the languages? I don't have to imagine it as I have been there and heard it, sitting in on the debates. Admittedly this was only the European Parliament, but it is a prototype of what

Inside the Brussels "puppet parliament."

the United Nations was trying to establish in New York in September 2000.

A parliament in which everyone hates everyone else and in which many of the delegates are security risks is a sad joke. This was the so-called Millennium Summit in New York, a political version of the earlier religious summit in which all faiths slapped each other on the back—when they weren't stabbing each other in the back, the pope having chosen this time to release a statement from a senior aid that "ours is the mother of churches." If you inserted the word "false" before churches, I would agree.

But to return to the mad, comical scene in New York, where thousands of police and security men were in attendance to stop many of the delegates getting holes blown in them . . .

Fidel Castro, that well known upholder of parliamentary democracy, arrived in a black limo at the Cuban Mission, no doubt to prepare a few thousand words on the meaning of peace and democracy . . . America had no choice but to grant the Cuban thug a visa, as a 1947 UN rule requires that the host country grant visas to those attending UN shindigs. Other windbags present ranged from Mugabe of Zimbabwe, fresh from encouraging racist attacks on the nation's white-owned farms, perhaps the only part of his economy still functioning efficiently, to Khatami of Iran. This grisly crew posed for pictures like some elderly high school reunion at the school of dictators. Then presidents, prime ministers and even the odd prince were to be given five minutes each to speak, with little red lights to tell the windbags when to stop. Outgoing President Clinton planned to use the event to browbeat Israel's Ehud Barak into ceding still more land to the terrorist Arafat, whose ambition, often stated, is to make Jerusalem the capital of Palestine. Clinton was joining his British clone Blair at a "third way" banquet, where the toast no doubt was the eradication of hunger.

The portentious—or should that be pretentious—three-day event ended with grand declarations about ending poverty, promoting education and democracy and, of course, the inevitable "fighting AIDS." The idea of fighting it by calling on people to sexually behave themselves and cease behaving promiscuously doesn't seem to have occurred to any delegates. Neither did dictators like Mugabe and Castro volunteer to help relieve poverty by repatriating their ill-gotten millions of looted money from foreign bank vaults. The calls for "respect for human rights" can be taken with large shovelfuls of salt, as the majority of leaders present were not elected democratically and welcome criticism or opposition about as much as Hitler or Stalin used to.

Supposing the good fairy—or more likely the bad fairy—made wishes come true, and the New World Order's planned parliament came out of this shambles, as at some stage in the near future it will. What would a world parliament be like? Let me take you back to Brussels, Belgium, and Strasbourg, France, where I have sat in on debates, or what passes for debates. The first thing that strikes anyone is that you cannot debate with people who don't understand your language. Pretty basic, this. To get round this problem there are rows of glass-fronted rooms round the debating chambers. Here sit hundreds of highly paid translators, doing simultaneous translations into the languages of Europe. French to German, German to English, and so on. It doesn't even begin to work. Say an MEP makes a joke in Italian. It may take a few seconds to translate this into Spanish. The Italian then gets serious and starts talking about funerals. Meanwhile the Spaniard has just heard the joke in his earphones and laughs. You get the picture.

When I was in Strasbourg, the parliament published a daily news sheet in about nine languages, with each language in a different colour paper. The publication was known as *The Rainbow*. This interested me, as I recalled reading Constance Cumbey's book *The Hidden Dangers of the Rainbow* which warned that New Agers and occultists had claimed this formerly Christian symbol as their own. Prior to being given a tour of the parliament, the group of journalists I was with was invited into an anteroom for a briefing. The lights went out, the screen lit up, and we saw a representation of the semicircular parliamentary chamber. In it the MEPs sit according to their political beliefs rather than their nationality, which in itself is interesting and significant. The voting blocks were identified by colours. On the far right, we had the deepest blue. On the left, rich red. In between were pinks, greens, and yellows. Then the commentator said: "And this is what happens when it all comes together." The screen shimmered, then all the colours merged, to form—a perfect rainbow. Their daily newsletter had a different color for each language of the community—and was collectively known as *The Rainbow*.

Back in New York it was a perfect muddle. The idea of winking red lights to curb each despot's hot air emission to just five minutes was never going to work. Castro is more used to five hours of windbaggery. However, some of the dictators on view met their match in New York's legendary lawyers, who probably did more to uphold peace and democracy than any delegate, by serving a summons on Chinese prime minister Li Peng, to appear before a judge in Manhattan to explain his role in the massacre at Tiananmen Square. This, of course, is only the massacre that the West knows about—there are ongoing repressions and tortures, particularly of Christians, although the liberal, Western press seldom mentions these. Anyway, Peng stormed home in a temper rather than face the judge, so removing one tyrant from the taxpayer-funded shindig. The blood-soaked president of the Sudan, another place where Christians are martyred regularly, many being crucified upside down, was also the lawyers' target, as was the hero of the Cuban revolution. No wonder Saddam Hussein and Colonel Gaddafi didn't show up—they would have needed to draft in emergency squads of lawyers from other cities to cope with demand. This wouldn't have been a new trend. When I visited a British site of an ancient castle, I was amused to see that the local baron travelled with fourteen lawyers—more than his number of knights!

It was interesting that diplomatic immunity did not seem to protect the despots, for the summons delivered to a guard outside Peng's suite at the Waldorf Astoria was ruled valid by a New York judge, creating possible problems if Peng should wish to return to America. The rest of the one hundred fifty-nine despots, kings, dictators, prime ministers, and presidents were mainly engaged in embassy entertaining after their "famous for five minutes" role in the spotlight, it can be assumed.

The next major event in the bid to say "goodbye nation state, hello superstate" was in December 2000, when leaders of the European Union met at Nice, France. And it wasn't nice at all for lovers of freedom and democracy as the trappings of a superstate were established, to rival the USA. It will eventually have a written constitution in which all issues will be decided by majority voting. Chris Patten, the European external affairs commissioner, said in April 2001 that the EU should use its power as the world's biggest aid donor to shape the international scene and "try to ensure that our political influence comes nearer to matching our economic weight." The EU will expand from its present fifteen members to include another thirteen countries, many of them formerly part of the Soviet Empire. Its judges will have power to strike down national laws. It will soon have its own strike force, a sixty thousand-strong highly mobile army led by Britain, France, and Germany.

This will be what a French paper called "flagrantly anti-American." The mystery, then, is why America's leaders have backed the

EU so fervently. Already there is a pan-European police force and soon there will be common policies in the fields of tax, defence, immigration, and just about everything else. NATO would cease to exist in its present form, as all major decisions would be taken in Brussels. Senators Smith and Helms wrote to the British press in December 2000, claiming that the Euro-army would risk undermining or even destroying the NATO alliance. This is, of course, the intention.

Conservative Shadow secretary of state Iain Duncan Smith MP, later Conservative leader, commented that this letter showed there is deep concern in the USA over the Euro-army and added: "The Nice agreement Tony Blair signed leaves the European Union in charge of the Euro-army, responsible for taking the operational decisions instead of NATO and making sure that NATO has no formal links with the Euro-army at any level. . . . He has risked the cohesion and effectiveness of NATO in a squalid attempt to curry favor with the French and other EU political leaders." Even Prince Charles said he was worried about the march to a Euro-army and its effect on Anglo/U.S. relations. Yet the amazing thing is how few people know all this, although all the details have been published. One now warning loud and clear is former British prime minister Margaret Thatcher, who was quoted on March 2, 2001, in the *Daily Telegraph* as saying the current prime minister, Tony Blair, must not betray the Americans over the rapid reaction force. She said transatlantic relations could break down.

The real danger at these international, globalist events is in what goes on behind the scenes, involving teams of officials and extragovernmental organisations with an agenda. Although the antics of the summit's politicians and those at Nice were reasonably well reported, you have to look further to find out the real purpose of this incredible gathering of powerful people. Scan the web, read obscure journals, get information from round the world, and read any serious-looking journal you can get your hands on—then you start to build the picture.

It was from *WorldNetDaily* columnist Jon E. Dougherty that I first learned of the world government meeting, which in time will be seen to have been much more important than it superficially seemed. His article was headed, "Major UN confab seeks to implement global decision-making world government." His story said the purpose was to examine the future of the world and "create an organisational structure whereby the peoples of the world can participate effectively in global decision making in the context of the United Nations system." The article stated that the Millennium Assembly and Summit was part of the UN's latest initiative to implement global government. The writer went on to say that a variety of influential nongovernmental organisations were paving the way for the meeting.

Already the language was becoming familiar to me and I was not surprised to see listed among these "important" organisations the World Federalist Association, an organisation I had previously been in touch with and which, assuming I was a supporter, had invited me as a delegate to its annual conference—in Baghdad. Other people in there pushing for a one-world government included Westminster United Nations Association, the One World Trust, the Commission for Global Governance, and the Royal Commonwealth Society. Addressed to "all the governments and peoples of the world they represent," these drum bangers urged every country to send representatives to New York—and most did.

I have enough documents from the world government enthusiasts to paper the walls of a sizeable college, so will spare you many of the intricate details. However, the plans have been worked out down to the tiniest detail—these people are *ready* and waiting! One

Publications of the World
Constitution and Parliament
Association now have a serious
input into UN future planning.

paper, headed *Manifesto*, describes its aims as: "For beginning world government with the ownership and management of all oceans and seabeds of earth." Approved at the fourth session of the Provisional World Parliament in 1996, it is published under the slogan "only one earth" by the World Constitution and Parliament Association, based in Colorado.

Inside, the manifesto states: "World Government begins with more than 70 percent of earth included!" After listing all the many things wrong with the world and its present governing bodies—all of them true—the one-worlders conclude: "Therefore the time has come for very decisive action to cut through the confusion and delay and establish positive direction to get the common affairs of the inhabitants of earth under responsible and democratic controls for the mutual and equitable benefit of everybody. This requires democratic federal world government." Sounds like Communism already, doesn't it?

The manifesto continues: "For this purpose a constitution for the Federation of Earth has already been prepared by delegates from all continents, working in four sessions of a World Constituent Assembly from 1968 to 1991. The Constitution for the Federation of Earth is ready for immediate ratification and implementation. . . ." The next bit is a little worrying, as it says that "we who are delegates from nongovernmental organisations . . . do hereby proclaim and take action." Acting "on behalf of all inhabitants of earth" they propose to "hereby take possession of all oceans and seabeds of earth from 20 kilometers offshore of all land masses and island territories of existing nation states, thus comprising at least 70 percent of earth for the beginning of world government. . . ." They also claim, on behalf of the earth's peoples, everything from the moon to Antarctica, airspace, stratospheric space, and lots more pie in the sky.

Having taken over the oceans and seabeds, and all the mineral rights, they would invite all nations and governments wanting to share in the benefits to join a world federation and ratify the Constitution for the Federation of Earth. Once they have hooked the world's politicians on this bait, they quickly reel them in. Next they send delegates to "the House of Nations of the World Parliament and arrange for elections to the House of Peoples." Both houses would convene as soon as twenty-five nations have ratified the constitution.

Step two is to rid the world of nuclear weapons "and all weapons of warfare." So they would outlaw the transport by sea or air—they have claimed dominion over both those—of all nuclear weapons and weapons of mass destruction, all other weapons for the conduct of war, soldiers, sailors, marines, ammunition, means of support for them, etc. Fines of an eye-wateringly severe nature would be levied on anyone breaking this embargo, so watch out, President Putin, you may have to go back to the World Bank and IMF for some more "loans."

Turning to money, there would be an Earth Financial Credit Corporation, created by pledging "the total wealth of the oceans and seabeds behind all creation of financial credit. . . . Revolving lines of credit shall be extended to each country or nation ratifying the Constitution for the Federation of Earth, on the basis of not less than one billion dollars for each million of population." This money "may be used in world trade wherever the new Earth Dollar accounting system is accepted." Their next step would be to tackle the entirely fictional "global warming" joke, although here they are a little behind the scientific times as the latest research from NASA, the American space agency, predicts instead a new ice age. Undeterred, our heroes would spend " a trillion dollars, or more, a year for the next 50 years, employing all available personnel." Presumably they would be walking round trying to persuade cows not to belch or emit "greenhouse gases" in other ways.

Next, in a cross between Penelope Pitstop and Superman, they would disarm the world, through the World Disarmament Agency, achieving universal immobilisation of armies, dismantling and elimination of nuclear weapons, or turning weapons systems over to peaceful uses "where practical." There would be a Global Energy Administration, Emergency Earth Rescue Administration, and so on, with "efficient low cost energy supplies" and all offshore oil wells closed down.

Their tenth provision is interesting. It reads: "For locations to carry out the administration of the terms of this Manifesto, and to begin the functions of the Provisional World Government, in conformity with Article XV of the Constitution for the Federation of Earth, we shall designate or direct the Presidium to designate areas within five continental areas of the earth as the first five Federal World Districts." Numbers are important in the Bible, which is always accurate. Dates and ages are given with precision, so if the world is being carved up into regions we have to take a look to see how it fits with prophecy. I have often wondered about the ten kings who will initially rule under Antichrist. They are unlikely to be kings in the literal sense as there are not ten significant kings left in the world with any power. In the West, most have nominal or ceremonial powers only.

What if the ten represent countries? This was an idea put forward as what was then called the Common Market was established in Europe, on May 9, 1950, in Paris, and the countries joining it rose from the initial six. However, soon there were twelve, then fifteen, and it became obvious that however the figures were juggled they would never be right. I have no doubt, however, that the revived Holy Roman Empire will be the seat of Antichrist, but that his rule will extend over all the world, as the Bible teaches. So the "ten" must be regions of the world. Will the capital be a "new Babylon," as many believe? All I know is that the city of Babylon is being rebuilt as I write, and that Iraq is a major enthusiast for the world government conferences it hosts each year.

Here I turn to the plans for world government, as discussed at the UN-sponsored Millennium Conference at New York in September 2000. I quote from a document headed "How World Government Will Work." For elections and administration, it states: "Earth is divided into 1000 districts, 20 regions, ten magna regions and at least five continental divisions." So there you have it. You live in one of the world's ten magna regions.

The main provisions of the world constitution are:

A world parliament comprised of three houses. A House of

Peoples, elected directly by the people equally from 1000 world electoral and administrative districts; a House of Nations, appointed or elected by national governments, and a House of Counsellors, 200 of them, elected by the other two houses. This has nominative, consultative, initiative and referral functions.

The World Executive, elected by and responsible to the parliament. A presidium of a rotating president and four vice presidents, all MPs. An executive cabinet of 30 ministers, all MPs. The World Executive may not veto or suspend the parliament or the constitution. There would be a world administration of about 30 departments, each headed by a cabinet minister or vice president, co-ordinated by a secretary general; chosen by the presidium and confirmed by the cabinet. The Integrative Complex includes agencies for world civil service, boundaries and elections; an institute on governmental procedures and world problems, research and planning, technological and environmental assessment, world financial administration and legislative review.

The would judiciary [will be] composed of eight benches having jurisdiction over different kinds of issues, with five continental seats. The collegium of world judges will be elected by parliament, headed by a presiding council of five members which assigns judges to the several benches.

To pause here so you can catch your breath, a world criminal court may be one of the first institutions to become reality. Britain has been one of the strongest advocates of such a court since it was approved by more than one hundred countries in a treaty in 1998. It will be set up under the auspices of the United Nations when sixty countries have ratified this treaty in their domestic parliaments. Over fourteen countries have ratified the treaty, including France, Italy, and Canada. Among just seven countries which opposed the treaty in 1998 were Israel, China, the USA, and India. America is worried that U.S. servicemen could be victims of politically motivated cases brought before the court and is unlikely to join under a Republican administration. However, if a huge majority of the UN members sign up, there are bound to be efforts to extend the reach of the court over the whole world, regardless of who has signed the treaty. One-world government has a great impetus behind it, as many people are about to find out.

Returning to the world government blueprint as discussed at the UN, I was intrigued by the section headed: "The enforcement system." This is what it says:

> Non military, it is headed by an office of world attorneys, elected by and removable by parliament. The world attorneys appoint the world police [removable by the parliament] to apprehend individual lawbreakers. . . . A world ombudsmus [sic] [would] protect human rights and ensure proper government functioning [and would be] headed by a council of five world ombudsen [sic] and commission of 20 regional world advocates, all elected by the parliament.

Can we rely on the fairness and impartiality of pan-national institutions, packed as they are by representatives from countries to whom democracy is an alien concept? What about if you come up against an "advocate" from Saudi Arabia or the Sudan, where they often advocate—and carry out—amputations as a punishment? Or what if your judge is from China, where their idea of free speech is to drag Christians out of meetings to chain and torture them, before forcing them into slave labour factories, assembling things like Christmas fairy lights for the American market? One American Baptist minister I met told me he personally knew such a man, forced by the thuggish Chinese authorities to make four thousand such lights each day. If he failed, he was beaten with a leather belt and starved.

The European Union, a prototype of the coming world government, is already homing in on religious freedom of speech and action. Here is what the Christian Institute of Britain has to say about a proposed "Employment Directive": "Who would have thought that a church or Christian organisation could be sued for refusing to employ an atheist or a practising homosexual? Yet leading lawyers have advised that this will be the effect of the proposed employment directive from the EU—and at least one EU commissioner has admitted it." The Christian Institute, based at 26, Jesmond Road, Newcastle upon Tyne, NE2 4PQ, England, says:

> The government is about to sign up to a European employment directive that could land religious groups in court. The directive would make it illegal for organisations to refuse to employ an individual because of that individual's religious views or sexual orientation. This means that religious groups could be forced to employ atheists or practising homosexuals in key positions in their organisations. Church schools will have to employ teachers who oppose the religious teachings of the denomination.
>
> All this represents a serious attack on religious liberty. . . . The UK government has already indicated its support for the employment directive. It is expected to be adopted by the Council of Ministers [the leading lights of the EU]. If it is adopted it immediately becomes law for public sector employment and must be fully implemented in the private sector by December 31, 2002.

The Christian Institute gives some interesting examples. The headmaster of a church school becomes a Muslim. The school dismisses him. The headmaster takes the school to an employment tribunal. The headmaster proves that his job did not involve teaching religious education. The tribunal finds that the school acted illegally in dismissing him for changing his religion. Or, another example could involve an evangelical youth organisation recruiting a full-time youth worker. When appointed, the youth worker was married, but she subsequently turns out to be a practising bisexual. The organisation feels unable to remove her from her position for fear of an expensive court order against them. The organisation would have no defence; the dismissal would undoubtedly be because of her "sexual orientation."

Here is another example, from the Institute's pamphlet "European Threat to Religious Freedom." A Christian Bible publishing business wants its Christian ethos to permeate all it does. A bright job interview candidate declares that he is "openly gay." If the firm rejects him in favor of another candidate, they fear a possible action for discrimination. The directive from the EU gives so-called "gay rights" precedence over religious freedoms. It gets worse. The burden of proof is on the defendant, as Article 9 of the directive requires that, in civil cases, employers will be assumed guilty of discrimination unless they can prove themselves innocent. At an employment tribunal, an employee will simply have to make out an allegation. If the employer cannot prove the allegation to be false, the tribunal will have to give judgment against them.

The Christian Institute concludes: "For religious groups this will mean even more time and money spent defending themselves in court—and more defeats." The directive also allows governments to make provision for positive discrimination in favor of groups that are perceived to be disadvantaged. This could mean, for example, "gay quotas," no doubt based on sodomites' own claims to be ten percent of the population. The true figure, according to the largest academic study of its kind ever carried out in the UK, has found, in the words of the Institute's comment "that only 0.3 of British men and 0.1 of women are exclusively homosexual. Employment policies under this proposal will become bogged down in statistics and gay rights propaganda." The survey was Wellings K et al "Sexual Behaviour in Britain," published by Penguin in 1994, page 209. Other surveys, even official government ones, have confirmed male homosexual figures of around one percent or less, and much less for women. This is despite a non-stop pro-homosexual barrage of favorable publicity and downright propaganda on television, night after night, no doubt put out by homosexual or ultraliberal television producers and executives. The "arts" is one of the professions to which they seem drawn.

Tony Pearce, director of the Messianic Testimony, a London-based outreach to the Jews, also edits a newsletter called *Light for the Last Days* at Box BM, 4226, London, WCIN 3XX. Tony is interviewed on my video, "End Times News: EU—Final World Empire," available in America from Hearthstone Publishing of Oklahoma City, Oklahoma, P.O. Box 100, Bethany, OK, 73008. It is available at $25 per copy (plus $4 post and packing) and is packed with two hours of vital information about the trend towards a one-world government headed by the Antichrist. Every Christian should have a copy to share with their unsaved—and saved—friends, relatives, and neighbors. In Britain the address is John Lewis, Woodside Farm, Lower Ham Lane, Elstead, Surrey,GU8 6HQ, and the price (including p and p) is £12.

In the April 1999 edition of his newsletter, Tony Pearce wrote:

> In the west "political correctness" means that Bible believing Christians who are opposed to sexual promiscuity, homosexual practice and abortion are the objects of scorn and derision from the "new establishment" who control the media and educational system. Many Christians are finding it increasingly difficult to hold down some jobs in the public sector because of demands that they accept antichristian moral values.

Channel 4, a British TV station, ridiculed the origins of Christianity in a broadcast one recent Christmas. However, it refused to give any Bible-believing Christian a right of reply, despite detailed criticisms of the program's absurdities from Tony Pearce, the offer of a debate and credible representations from other Christians including myself.

Jesus said that one of the signs of the last days would be worldwide persecution. Matthew 24: 9 says: "Then shall they deliver you up to be afflicted, and shall kill you: and ye shall be hated of all nations for my name's sake." In many countries of the world this is already happening, with estimates of Christian martyrs ranging up to a quarter of a million a year, although the true total is impossible to know. In countries from China to Sudan terrible fates await anyone caught worshipping the Lord Jesus. In the West at present we mostly just face derision and hostility, although the hatred of fundamentalist Christians is growing fast. I know this, in part, from the hate mail I get if I mention anything supporting Jesus, or the Bible, in a newspaper. It is also quite interesting that much of the hostile mail comes from people who call themselves Christians, followers of the Alpha course, and so on—people who are ecumenical in mindset.

There was a particularly illuminating article in Britain's *Daily Telegraph* newspaper. The article was headed: "Mentor's message: stay on the Third Way." The story was about Britain's premier Blair getting advice from the man described as his spiritual mentor, Catholic theologian Hans Kung.

The article, printed on July 21, 2000, stated: "Speaking from his hilltop home, the Catholic scholar has advised Mr. Blair to draw strength from his beliefs in his hour of need." The article says that Kung's "pursuit of a global ethic" has greatly impressed Blair. "Prof. Kung believes politicians should play a vital role in advancing the global ethic," according to the article. The friendship between the two men has flourished since the prime minister invited Prof. Kung to his home after reading his best-seller, *On Being a Christian*. The theologian also believes that harmony and peace between religions is the key to world peace, an idea which is giving impetus to the fast-moving "churches together" organisation, just one of the ways in which the seeds of the one-world church, the great whore church, are being sown. The professor has not always brought Tony Blair the best results, however. After making a silly and muddled speech to Prof. Kung's Global Ethics Foundation in Germany, in which Blair advocated on-the-spot fines for drunken louts on Britain's streets, within a few days his son, Euan Blair, sixteen, had been found the worse for drink in Leicester Square, London.

There is a strong religious element to the coming New World Order. If we have political world unity, we must also have religious unity, as religious conflicts have often caused major wars in the past. So everywhere, in the twenty-first century, the talk is of "churches together," "the ecumenical movement," and "all roads lead to God." This is Satan's oldest lie—he has no new tricks as the old ones continue to work so well.

Chapter 10

Standardising the World

The one-worlders plan to unify the world's weights and measures, including temperature measurements. What could be stranger, for example, than the fact that the English-language programs of the Discovery Channel, aired in Britain and America, constantly quote measurements in meters, kilometers, kilograms, and so forth, despite the fact that ninety percent of their target audience would not clearly understand what they were talking about? I have called the station and written to them in protest, without receiving an answer.

My guess is that they cannot give a good one! All over Britain and America road signs use miles. Yet Discovery always uses kilometers. I do not know anybody, not even teenagers, who ever gives a distance in kilometers. So why, *why*, when you are making programs for English speakers, deliberately use foreign measurements? The BBC, the most treacherous of national broadcasters with values alien to the majority of its listeners, follows the one-worlders' line by indoctrinating listeners and viewers with the idea that all measurements must be metric. They long ago gave up using Fahrenheit for temperatures, again despite the fact that Fahrenheit is what most of us are familiar with. Why? What possible reason could there be, other than a one-world agenda?

That the authorities are determined to use extreme steps to stamp out Imperial measures is shown in the case of the "Metric Martyr," an English greengrocer convicted in court for selling a pound of bananas. His lawyer, Michael Shrimpton, said the trial of

Prosecuted for selling a pound of bananas! Freedom in the new Reich of Europe.

Steven Thoburn was "the most controversial" prosecution in England since the seventeenth century Witchcraft Act was used to have women suspected of witchcraft burned at the stake or hanged. Mr. Shrimpton, a constitutional barrister, said it was the first time in three hundred years that an innocent person had been brought before a court to face such a discredited law.

The courtroom in Sunderland, northeast England, was packed to see the small-time businessman, who sells fruit and vegetables from a market stall, hauled into the dock charged with the terrible crime of selling a bunch of bananas weighed in pounds and ounces. The Trading Standards officers of Sunderland Council decided to make an example of Mr. Thoburn for daring to defy European dictates about going metric. His lawyer, Mr. Shrimpton, said the European Commission was determined to make Britain metric by compulsion, whereas British governments had in the past allowed freedom of choice between metric and imperial. In 1994 a law was introduced bringing in compulsory metrication when a minister signed regulations allowing a European directive to become British law. A five-year changeover period was allowed but, on the stroke of midnight on December 31, 1999, it became illegal for traders to

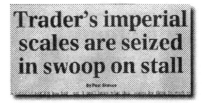

More on Britain's top criminal.

sell loose goods in pounds and ounces.

Mr. Thoburn denied two charges of using unmetricated scales and he could have gone to jail or been fined up to $3,000. After he was found guilty of using scales calibrated for imperial measures only, he was given a conditional discharge. His scales were confiscated and the bad news is he may have to pay legal charges which could rise well into six figures, depending how far he appeals to higher courts. Steven's supporters think the case shows just how far British law has been undermined by European law. For Steven is seen by the authorities as a threat to the European Union, so an example must be made of him. His lawyer says there is no reason the two sets of measures cannot be used side by side: "For one hundred thirty-six years the policy of Britain has been freedom of choice." He also says the European Union has no powers to override Britain's national laws which state, in the 1985 Weights and Measures Act, that dual measurements will be allowed.

This was not a case about a bunch of bananas. It was—and continues to be, as Steven is now to appeal the ruling—about who actually rules Britain, the people who elect MPs to make their laws or a bunch of unelected and sometimes crooked commissioners—or commissars—in Brussels. Because the superstate is greedy for power and the abolition of the nation state, an honest man has been in the dock, while they have freed hundreds of terrorists and murderers from jail in Northern Ireland. The authorities mean business—expensive business. To convict this one small-time trader they are spending £200,000 in order to "protect the public." Yet nobody is on record as asking for protection from Steven Thoburn and his bananas. In a truly free country, any-

'A kilo of pound weights, please'

This cartoon caption reads: "A kilo of pound weights, please."

one confused by the greengrocer's allegedly outdated weights could take their trade elsewhere.

In fact, Mr. Thoburn did have a set of metric scales in his shop, for anyone who wished to buy in kilograms. Only one customer ever did so. However, when Judge Bruce Morgan gave his verdict at Sunderland Magistrates' Court in April, 2001, the fifty-page ruling went entirely against Mr. Thoburn. The judge argued for the primacy of European law since Britain joined the then-European Economic Community in 1972. Constitutional barrister Michael Shrimpton, who defended the greengrocer, is now appealing for funds to take the fight further. However, £100,000 is needed just to fund the defendant's costs, and while volunteers are fighting for freedom, the huge weight of the state and its mighty resources are against Steven.

At the time of going to press, money was coming in from all over the world to fund an appeal. Said Mr. Shrimpton: "I am confident the British public will be alarmed by the terms of the judgment and the way the sovereignty of Parliament can be undermined by a European directive." The scales of justice, be they imperial or metric, seem to be turning against freedom lovers and supporters

'I want you to imagine that hut is a greengrocer's selling vegetables in pounds and ounces'

"Sarge, I think these scales are in pounds and ounces."

More cartoons pointing out the absurdity of the ban on imperial measures.

of the nation state. However, Steven Thoburn said the support he has received from thousands of ordinary British people had convinced him he must carry on the fight. He is to appeal against his conviction. The Conservative Party's then leader, William Hague, signalled his support. Events proceed as we go to press.

In June 2001 came news of two more heroes stepping forward to challenge the metric madness. Like Steven, they are clearly arch criminals(!) Traders John Dove and Julian Harman faced the magistrates at Bodmin Magistrates Court in Cornwall, in the far west of England. They were before the court for selling brussels sprouts, apples, and fish in pounds and ounces. This is one sprout of freedom that Brussels intends to crack down on. Mr. Harman, a forty-two-year-old greengrocer, is accused of selling sprouts for thirty-nine pence to the pound and Granny Smith apples at forty-five pence per pound. Mr. Dove, a fifty-two-year-old fishmonger, is accused of selling a fish called pollack for £3.28 a pound and mackerel for £1.54 a pound. The other charges against them relate to selling goods in imperial measures and one each of obstructing Cornwall County Council trading standards officer Sharon Foster.

Mr. Harman said that since the first week of last year he had returned to selling goods in pounds and ounces. He went metric for a week and lost £300 in takings as people thought his goods were more expensive. "I'm a small trader—I can't afford to lose £300 in a week," he said. No customers had asked for goods in metric—"they all want their goods in pounds and ounces." Mr. Dove, who runs J. Dove Fishmongers, said that ninety-nine percent of his customers supported his stand: "My job is to serve the public. They are the ones who should dictate how things are served."

This case is also on its way to higher courts and already freedom's defenders have raised £200,000 to fight the legal battles, together with those of Steven Thoburn and that of another small shopkeeper, in London.

Stealth is being used to make sure Britain is less and less a "free country." All imperial measures will be banished from shop shelves in Britain by December 31, 2009, after which Britain's shopkeepers won't be allowed to show prices in pounds and ounces alongside metric equivalents. The Department of Trade and Industry set the date in what critics called "a hidden deadline," which few knew about and which was not debated in Parliament. Using an obscure parliamentary device, the new rule says after 2009 all imperial measures must go, except the mile, the acre, the pint for draught beer and milk, and troy ounces for precious metals. Vivian Linacre, director of the British Weights and Measures Association, which fights to save the traditional measures, commented: "European Union officials have admitted to me their real motivation is to remove Britain's 'unfair' advantage over the rest of Europe in terms of trade with America, where pounds, ounces and gallons remain predominant."

Britain's weights and measures evolved naturally over thousands of years. The foot is an obvious, convenient measure to use and I have often paced out distances in buildings to get a rough idea of how many "feet" the floor measured. The acre first appeared during the reign of Ethelbert II, King of Kent, from A.D. 560 to 616. A yard was introduced in the reign of King Henry I, from 1100 to 1135, when it was said to be the distance between the king's nose and his outstretched arm. An inch was the width of a thumb. An agreement on a standard set of weights and measures was part of the Magna Carta in 1215, the birth of modern parliamentary democracy. How interesting that it was the would-be Holy Roman emperor Napoleon who decided that metres were the rational way forward and scrapped all the time-honored ways of measuring. Anyone who thinks that the metre is a rational measurement should know that its length was defined in 1791 by the French Academy of Sciences. They said it was to be 1/10,000,000 of the quadrant of the earth's circumference running from the North Pole via Paris (of course!) to the Equator.

As I write, the case of the metric martyr may yet be overturned by a higher court. Just maybe, the EU juggernaut will skid to a halt on a banana skin. Meanwhile greengrocer Steven and his supporters have tried to cheer themselves up by going out for a meal—of quarterpounder burgers! Give some people an inch and they take a mile . . .

Chapter 11

The Spies in the Sky

As commuters walk through town to catch their trains to work, their movements are filmed and recorded. On the subway, every wall and pillar bristles with electronic equipment. At journey's end, electronic eyes follow their progress into offices where at reception desks they show electronic passes and go to the elevators, tracked by more cameras. Fifty-four years ago, George Orwell wrote *1984*, a novel about a horrific future in which the government spied on every aspect of a citizen's life. He envisaged a Big Brother figure monitoring our movements. The date he chose at random was a reversal of the year in which he wrote the book. But George wasn't

Spy cameras in a typical British housing estate in Berkshire, England.

far out. Now, in the twenty-first century not only is Big Brother watching
you—so is everyone else.

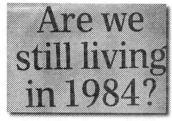

Are we still living in 1984?

A reference to the book title, which also inspired the catchphrase, "Big Brother is watching you."

Walk through a large British city
and you are watched, on average, by
three hundred cameras on thirty different systems. Britain is the most
watched society in the world, with
over two and a half million surveillance cameras, a number that is
growing fast. George envisaged big government keeping an eye on
us, but in the twenty-first century everybody is in on the act, from
big business to local government. Yet surveys reported in the *London Daily Mail* of March 7, 2001, show that two-thirds of the public
don't even know they are being watched and recorded, every-
where from their local newsagents to McDonalds.

Perhaps there is little surprise in this, for many of the cameras
are "pinhole" types, under a square inch in area. In 1998, 125,000
of these were sold in Britain and as you read this they are out there
somewhere—watching, on everything from London red buses to
cash machines. The new generation of cameras can even pick up
sound! Motorists who stray into London's bus-only lanes can find

The famous picture of Big Brother inspired by George Orwell's book *1984* about a future totalitarian state where everyone is watched.

themselves receiving a fine through
the post—as those no longer friendly
red leviathans use spy cameras to
watch for motoring infringements.

Surveillance has spread from the
big cities, through the small country
towns, and is now out in the tiny villages. In America, a forest ranger told
me it has gone further than that—
there are cameras in the deepest forests, ostensibly to watch for forest
fires. That may be their purpose for
the present . . .

When our son Daniel and I went
out and about in the district of Hart,

Local Member of Parliament Nick Hawkins with other civic dignitaries at the launch of a camera surveillance system in Camberley, Surrey, England.

Hampshire, England, to film a segment on surveillance cameras for our video *EU: Final World Empire*, we were surprised at how many camera locations we found, even outside country pubs in the middle of villages. The funniest thing that happened was when one of the cameras zoomed in on us as we were filming it! Of course, there is a "good reason" for all this.

As Christianity has been kicked out of the country, lawlessness has flooded in, so the cameras are supposedly there to deter people from committing crime. Every time I have been present when a surveillance room has opened in one of our local towns, the message has been "this will cut crime." There is obviously some truth in this, as serious criminals are unlikely to commit crime in full view of cameras, although drunken hooligans often don't seem to care. From the control rooms you can zoom in on every part of the town center, watch without being watched. As I step out of my Hampshire office I look up and there is the all-seeing eye in the sky. When I wrote the newspaper headline after they were installed, I called them "sky spies."

What has often been argued is that the cameras displace crime, sending miscreants off to darker corners in which to do their criminal deeds. Certainly you can drive round back streets of local towns where I work and watch drug dealers at work, away from surveillance.

Cameras can be a boon to the law abiding and often do assist the police. The other day, an oddball made a nuisance of himself in our newspaper's reception area and refused to leave. We called the police, who told us when they arrived that they had seen him on their surveillance equipment as he left our offices and walked up the road.

Britain is the closed circuit capital of the world. The average resident could be filmed on up to thirty different systems in one day in a typical large British city.

Another town expands its sky spy system. This time it's Fleet, Hampshire. Delegations from around the world have visited to see how it works prior to introducing it themselves.

There are now systems in place in London which enable you to scan in pictures of "most wanted" people or undesirables, and the cameras will pick them out.

People passing the one hundred forty-four security cameras in the East London borough of Newham have their faces checked automatically against a video library of known criminals. If the system recognises a criminal "face" the security officers at the control room in East Ham call the nearest police station. The police can then watch the suspect on a screen in their own police station to see whether they wish to take action against them. Malcolm Smith, environment director for Newham Council, said: "We have pushed this technology further than anyone else. Once the police have been alerted they can decide if the person is a shoplifting threat, a burglary threat, or whatever. The system is about crime prevention. For example, if a known shoplifter is seen coming out of East Ham subway station, the staff at local stores can be put on alert."

Some civil liberties groups are alarmed at this development, but Mr. Smith said that the civil liberties he was interested in were those of people wishing to go about their lawful business in Newham without being bothered by anybody. The system is sophisticated enough to take into account the angle of a person's head, whether they are wearing eye-glasses, make-up, or earrings; their facial expression, the light conditions, and even the aging process. Only the

This amusing cartoon is from the *Daily Mail*, London. It shows a man creeping along, careful to avoid all the spy cameras on every street corner. He thinks he's made it—but the shop proprietor has a pinhole camera in his buttonhole!

police know whose identities are stored in the database. All this is fine as long as the forces of law and order are relatively benevolent and "on our side." Britain's home secretary—the law and order minister—had this to say: "In effect we have traded some of our rights to privacy in public places for increased security. Most of us think this is a price worth paying" (*Daily Telegraph*, May 13, 1999). Many citizens who live in town centres can be filmed from the minute they leave their front gate, often by hidden cameras. It is this passive acceptance of all these cameras that is, perhaps, the most frightening thing of all. Soon cameras will not be bolted on to buildings, they will be designed in from the start, as integral parts of the structure.

Not only are our images to be scanned, our numbers soon will be as well. On June 26, 1997, the British government sparked another civil liberties row by announcing plans to give every child in the country a national identification number at the age of four, in order, they said, to plot children's progress throughout their school careers. New central records will enable officials to track pupils from school to school to measure their progress at each stage. However, civil liberties campaigners immediately pointed out that the system could pave the way for national identity cards, something the Labor government opposed when in opposition. David Hawker, who is developing the scheme for the School Curriculum and Assessment Authority, said: "We are looking at setting up a national pupil number. It is nothing to be frightened of because pupil information is covered by the Data Protection Act. Local education authorities already have their own numbering systems."

The terrorist atrocities in America have brought renewed calls in both countries for all citizens to carry identity cards. When it is realised that these can be lost, stolen, or forged, the next step will be the mark on our bodies, containing every detail of our lives. The world will finally be in Big Brother's grip.

Andrew Puddephat, director of the civil rights pressure group Charter 88, said: "Once you have a unique identification number to keep track of pupils you really have the basis for an identity card system. It is a cliché to talk about a slippery slope, but who knows how it could be used? The government must explicitly rule out any extension of its use for other purposes." John Wadham, the director of Liberty also spoke of "the downside of serious civil liberties implications."

Personal identity cards for every adult Briton are also part of the government's planned electronic revolution. There are good reasons. Benefit fraud is rampant, as are scams of every kind, usually directed at lax government departments. Cards enabling people to claim social security benefits, which would also carry details of their tax affairs, health records, and so on, would make fraud more difficult. A "government source" has been quoted as saying: "The potential scope for the new card is huge. We do not wish to impose the card or to intimidate people with fear of Big Brother. But the idea is that everyone would have one. It would become an important card because it would be so useful." Tony Blair's think tank, the Performance and Innovation Unit, is to recommend the introduction of the cards which will have a unique personal identifier - such as a thumbprint.

The plan was published in 2001 and will probably become government policy. A sort of "backdoor identity card," it will feature a microchip containing a range of personal details. One government source quoted in the British press said that the next step could be genetic ID cards, containing details of each person's DNA. Already the police have been given powers to keep indefinitely DNA samples taken from innocent people. The way for the introduction of the card is being prepared by talk that they would solve the problem of insecure credit cards on the Internet. Use of soft phrases like "empowering the citizen" will calm the fears of the nervous. And as newspapers report that each day more and more illegal immigrants vanish on arrival and more and more money is lost to fraud and other crime, currently costing Britain £60 billion a year, the call for the cards will become stronger.

A potentially sinister proposal passed almost unnoticed after I spotted it in the *Times* of April 2, 1998, headed: "Cameras to scan for stolen cars." The story told of plans for a police super-computer able to screen millions of vehicles on motorways for stolen cars. It said that by 2003 cameras on main road networks, key junctions, tunnels, and all ports and airports will be linked to an enlarged police national computer sited at Hendon in North London. As vehicles pass the cameras their registration numbers will be automatically read against Britain's forty-five million national registration records and a file of two hundred thousand stolen or suspect vehicles.

The report said that the new system will look through files in seconds and alert traffic police to intercept or follow suspect vehicles. The system has already been tested in the City of London's "ring of steel" defences against future IRA attacks and at the ports of Dover and Stranraer. The Police Information Technology Organisation, which runs the computer, has signed the multimillion pound contract for the new equipment. The report closes by saying that the vehicle check system has already been used by British police forces and has produced an arrest in one big case.

For those of us who have ever had a vehicle stolen, this seems like a wonderful advance. There are few things more frustrating than returning to where your car had been left, only to find it missing. This has just happened to a friend, days before he was due to meet a well known international minister due for a lecture tour of Britain. The car was found two weeks later, badly damaged and with another two thousand miles on the clock, at the other end of

Volvo On Call
October 2000

VOLVO

A vehicle tracking device, which comes as an option on new Volvos.

Britain. It was used by fraudsters operating a scam involving false documents. So not many of us are going to say: "Wait a minute, what about the implications for privacy?" We just want our property kept safe and, of course, we want to back the police in their efforts.

Helping motorists whose vehicles have broken-down is another positive aspect of satellite tracking. A friend reported that when he called for help he was told not only where his car was situated but also that he had pulled into a field! In October 2001, a fleet of camera cars was introduced in Britain that scan cars' licence plates as they drive past, instantly comparing them with a computer database to catch out tax dodgers. But a broader brush can be seen at work behind the immediate anti-crime and vehicle recovery factors. The all-seeing eye of George Orwell's *1984* is much closer than we think.

Farmers in Britain have already found that their remotest fields are not safe from prying eyes. I know of a farmer, not far from where I live in Hampshire, who decided that he would take part in the "set aside" scheme under which you are paid for leaving your land fallow, or unplanted. The reason is to reduce the food mountains for which Europe has become notorious because of the workings of the Common Agricultural Policy. One day he had been mowing his lawn and left his lawnmower out in one of the nearby fields. Within a few days he was amazed to get a telephone call from officials at the Ministry of Agriculture, Fisheries and Food. They wanted to know why he had "agricultural equipment" out in a field which he was not supposed to be farming.

It seemed that the farmer had been spied on by satellite and reported to the enforcers at the ministry. He ended up in some trouble and with a hefty fine to pay, a story I recount on my video where I filmed right in front of the farm where this happened. On another occasion the same farmer was laying in some logs for the winter in one of his empty, open sided barns. This, too, was spotted from a satellite and the inquiry came: "Why is there commercial activity in your barn? You are not supposed to be farming." Again, no mercy was shown and the farmer was fined. I cannot name him, because the red tape merchants have got people so scared they are fearful of retribution if they stir up trouble.

On another occasion I was in the Isle of Wight, an island off the southeast coastline of England, when a farmer told me of a similar interesting incident. One day a call had come through to his farmhouse, from a man at the ministry. He said: "Your field in the northeast corner of your farm is ready for cropping." It seems that satellite surveillance is now so detailed that the ripeness of crops can easily be detected from space. The farmer was not complaining—he was glad of the advice. However, it does indicate how closely our activities can be monitored, however "remote" our homes or businesses appear to be.

Will cameras next be required inside our homes? People may laugh, but I think this is entirely likely. Under the emerging Socialist superstate of Europe legions of new laws are spewing forth, many of them relating to "equality." Well, are you brainwashing your children at home? Are you dutifully presenting your daughters with diggers and trucks and your boys with dolls, just to ensure there is no gender pressure to conform to role stereotypes? Is each religion being given a fair hearing? Worst of all, are your children being told the unthinkable, that there is one God and Jesus is the way to Him? Big Brother wants to know about this, put a stop to it and, perhaps soon, order your children to be taken away from such unsuitable parents, so they can be brainwashed into good little one-worlders who know that "people" are the enemy of "Mother" (earth). All this is already happening in many schools, so there is no reason to think it won't be extended to homes.

A campaigner named David Burke recently wrote a book called *Spy TV* and spent a year interviewing the people behind the digital TV revolution. He says that what they were most excited about was "the new ability of this technology to create experimental conditions in the home." He added: "Your interactive TV set will be able to show you something, monitor your reactions, and then show you something else. It is a cycle of stimulus, response, and measurement that is used on lab rats in laboratory experiments." The idea is that, having established what a viewer likes, broadcasters can then set about trying to manipulate it—getting people watching longer and buying more. Privacy laws could be used to limit surveillance in the home, but few privacy campaigners believe the politicians

Forget Big Brother, it's your TV watching you

Articles describing how interactive television is monitoring viewers' preferences.

will take on media moguls.

Have you ever thought how supermarkets and other stores are also building a vast dossier on your buying habits? Store "loyalty" cards are not just there to encourage you to stick with your store, they are also intended to build up a file on your purchasing habits. Already some stores in America are noting your buying and, if they have offers they think will interest you, call you to let you know.

I often think that the scenes described in wartime Holland, where Jewish refugees from the Holocaust like Anne Frank were hidden in secret rooms, could not happen in any future scenario where a minority was being hunted down. The fact that Mrs. Franklin had doubled her milk purchase for the week would be immediately noted and arouse instant suspicion.

You might think the government would not want to know how many cans of beans we buy in a week. You would be wrong. The *Daily Mail* of London reported on January 25, 1999, that the British government had asked supermarkets to hand over the records of loyalty card holders. The supposed reason given was that the government's health experts could then compare the eating habits of thirty million cardholders and their families to see if eating genetically modified foods caused illness. I would have been more inclined to believe this had I not heard the prime minister on radio shortly before this, stating that hardly any foods in Britain had GM ingredients! So there must have been another reason . . .

If Big Brother wanted to see who was likely to have rebellious leanings against the one-world superstate, they could even note from our checked out library books who had certain political or religious leanings—or was simply of an independent mind. Very little is secret in the age of the computer chip and smart card, for an adult in the developed world is located, on average, on three hundred databases. As these converge, and as computers are increasingly able to talk to one another, nearly all of us are becoming entangled in a web of surveillance encompassing everything from our bank balances to our e-mails, our library book records to our children's school grades. Few people currently fear this intrusion of authority into their supposed privacy, only becoming dimly aware of it when they receive unexpected phone calls from people trying to sell them things. These calls are not random: they are made by companies who build up dossiers on likely sales subjects, based on past behaviour and preferences.

A top British government official shocked privacy campaigners in December 2000 when he revealed plans to get details of every move made by every citizen—and store them for seven years, a figure that ties in uncomfortably with the length of the coming Great Tribulation. Roger Gaspar, deputy director general of the National Criminal Intelligence Service, wrote a document on behalf of the police, customs, secret services, and GCHQ, the spy center located at Cheltenham where forty-five hundred employees, mostly mathematicians and linguists, crack codes and listen in on conversations on behalf of the British and American governments.

Mr. Gaspar wants details of every phone call, e-mail, fax, and website visit made available to the authorities and stored for up to seven years. According to a report in the *Daily Mail* of December 4, 2000, the authorities would be able to search the data for information on law-breakers. The paper says the document from Gaspar is said to claim that the proposals are vital for tackling "cybercrime," terrorism, drug trafficking, and pornography rings. Part of the plan would be to set up a vast data warehouse to store the information on the ultimate Big Brother computer system, costing $39 million a year to operate. At present the proposals are being looked at "very seriously" according to a spokesman for the Home Office. Predictably, civil libertarians are not so enthusiastic, with Deborah Clark of Liberty saying: "We would view this as a massive intrusion into personal privacy." The Conservatives' Lord Cope commented that the powers sought could "quickly slip into the world of Big Brother."

We are often trapped—or forced—into revealing massive amounts of private and personal details even when we wish to fill out forms to cover guarantees on pots and pans. How old are you, how many in your family, how old are they, where do you live, what do you earn, and so on? I recently received a "postal preference" form of staggering complexity. Under the guise of helping cut out unwanted mailshots, it sought to find out the most intimate details of our lives. I returned it, of course. Inside, across the myriads of intrusive questions, I wrote one large message: "Mind your own business!" Many people do gullibly fill in these documents. This information is then sold to people like life insurance salesmen who target their victims from lists of likely prospects. Credit agencies, local government with its electoral registers, and all kinds of private bodies gladly sell the information forced out of us.

One of the Trafficmaster blue cameras that monitor every main road in Britain, recording number plates. This one is outside the firm's British headquarters.

There is a successful firm in Britain called Trafficmaster. I have written about them and filmed them in their spectacular, futuristic control room. This is a fine company, run by innovative people, and I wish I held some of their shares. What is Trafficmaster? It's a company which monitors the movement of vehicles. As you drive round Britain you may have noticed frequent blue poles with cameras on the top. Their cameras also dangle from virtually every motorway bridge. They can report to companies exactly where their vehicles are, the speed they have done between two points, and so on. They currently film only part of each number plate but there is no technical reason why they couldn't take in the whole number. Another firm offers companies a device called Tracker,

Inside Trafficmaster's control room.

now being widely fitted to company cars, which plots the driver's every move. This system is being offered throughout the world at present.

A rival company, called Minorplanet, supplies "vehicle management information" products which, when fitted "discreetly" to vehicles provide live tracking via satellite, as well as detailed journey reports. So, if you are a company rep on the road, no more crafty halts for cups of tea or chats with friends! Big Brother will know all about it! Minorplanet has a partnership with America's

Electronic spies fitted in fleet company's cars

A *Financial Times* headline about the "spy in the car" system.

giant GE Capital Fleet Services and this device, which is clearly aimed at letting bosses snoop on their drivers, will soon be in an American vehicle near you. Their business in the year 2000 increased by one hundred sixty-five percent, so clearly a lot of firms are signing up for the spy in the cab.

One of the latest Renault cars offers companies the facility to simply download every detail of the driver's journeys, their time, the stops, the mileage etc. This is increasingly likely to become the norm. As well as tracking devices within cars and by outside agencies, the likely introduction of electronic road tolls on Britain's main highways will provide another means of monitoring and controlling people.

Britain's deputy prime minister, John Prescott, said on June 28, 1999, that he intends to press ahead with controversial plans for road tolls. Trials were launched in the cities of Leeds and Edinburgh to test electronic charging equipment. The stated aim is to "cut congestion," although the obvious way to do this—by building some decent roads in Britain—isn't even being considered. The trials of electronic charging systems started at the end of 2000. This system, if adopted, will mean that every driver's movement is recorded electronically as their swipe cards are processed by roadside devices. Similar systems are already in use in America, in places like Boston, Massachusetts, where the turnpike system is paid for by road tolls. Drivers there still have the choice of paying by cash or cards, so it is still possible to cruise up the pikes anonymously by proffering cash. For the present.

Several American states have accused the federal government of duping them into allowing pictures of millions of citizens to be gathered in a new computer database which, they feared, could be used to track people moving round the country. The system was set up to help storekeepers fight fraud and was also promoted as a weapon against illegal immigration and terrorism. The state governments involved sold driving licence photographs to Image Data,

a New Hampshire company which markets fraudbusting computers to be sited near shop tills. A tamper-proof picture of the credit
card or chequebook owner appears on the screen, helping cut crime.
However, Congress put $1.5 million into the project as the Secret
Service's contribution for technical support, raising fears that government wants to keep tabs on its citizens for reasons other than
retail fraud. In other words, Big Brother could use the system to
keep an eye on people with political opinions it didn't like, as well
as people deemed extreme or dangerous—like fundamentalist Christians, for example. I have already been told that government agencies in America monitor the phone calls and websites of campaigning Christian organisations that keep an eye on plans for one-world
government. It is relatively easy to track where the "hits" on your
site are coming from . . .

You may already be watched in more unlikely places. The Illi-
nois Power Company wasn't trying to violate anyone's privacy when
it set up videotape equipment to find out who was vandalising a
restroom at its Clinton nuclear power station, according to company officials. However, the *St. Louis Post-Dispatch* of May 8, 1999,
reported that eight male workers filed a suit that alleged they were
secretly videotaped while inside the bathroom stalls and showers.
The company's corporate counsel, Brad Johnson, said that the firm
operated within the boundaries of the law and had notified the
sheriff, the Nuclear Regulatory Commission, and the union stew-
ard. He also said the vandalism stopped after taping started.

Employees in call centres are routinely spied upon, with their
electronic supervisors monitoring how long they take dealing with
each customer, how effective they are, and even how many lavatory breaks they take. George Orwell would immediately recognise
their work environment and that of almost any computer-based
company in the world today.

Surveillance can start at your office computer. We use a newspaper page make-up system called Miles 33, based around software called QuarkExpress and Scribe. It notes when every journalist logs on, what they are writing, how long it takes, and so on.
It has a feature called an audit trail. If, say, someone at a distant

head office wished to find out who was writing on, for example, religion, they could request the system to throw up all stories on religion, who wrote them, what they were about, how many words they were, where they were used, and everything else about them. Everything you keyboard can be logged and permanently recorded. It's potentially a control-freak's delight.

Suppose you use your office computer to send e-mails to friends. Many people regularly e-mail friends and relatives from work, book seats at theaters, or log on to web sites. In a small way this seems relatively harmless; most people do it. However, there is also serious abuse. Many people log on to pornography sites or just waste time e-mailing jokes around the world.

I know a web service provider who for operational reasons occasionally had to look into all the traffic passing through his firm's servers. In other words, he had to snoop—technically very easy. He said that eighty-five percent of the supposedly work-related traffic was in fact rubbish, mostly dirty jokes and cartoons being sent out to hundreds of people. This was what had used up all the system's capacity on one occasion. A dirty old man? Actually, it was a young girl who was responsible.

My friend became familiar with the traffic into some of his customers' sites and said that the most urgent item awaited by one managing director was details of an angling contest he was entering! It is easy to see why employers want to stop the waste of time and money, so in Britain, firms now have legal rights to look in on their employees' e-mails. They are increasingly using them. As I write, one local controversy concerns three women sacked after they sent an allegedly offensive cartoon by e-mail, something they strongly deny. It turned out there was no hiding place for what they thought was a private joke. Of course, anyone who knew their passwords could have sent the e-mail, and they would get the blame.

These powers to snoop were introduced after heavy lobbying from employers' organisations. So they can hardly complain that the government wanted to get in on the act. The British government has passed something called the Regulation of Investigatory Powers Act. This forces all internet service providers to install, at their expense, a black box linked to the headquarters of M15, Britain's counterintelligence service. This means that the secret service and other government authorities can read the e-mail of everyone using those service providers. The new act also means government agencies can make firms hand over their confidential encryption keys, which code electronic data. If the government wishes to spy on a company, it allegedly has to serve notice on a senior member of that company. However, apart from watching for e-mails which relate to criminal activity or national security, which many would not quarrel with, the law now means government can listen in on firms "for the purpose of safeguarding the economic well-being of the UK." That casts a pretty wide net.

Even mobile phones can be tracked, and now that over half the population of Britain uses them, 30.6 million people as of October 2000, maybe more of us should realise that they can be used as electronic tags, pinpointing our whereabouts, even long after we have left any one location. As far back as 1995 there was the first successful prosecution based on mobile phone surveillance following police inquiries into the shooting of three Essex drug dealers. The killers were tracked through their use of mobile phones. Police found that when

TRACKER Communicator and BT Cellnet offer WAP based solution services and monitoring service to customers

This is not just a mobile phone; it is a tracker device which pinpoints and monitors drivers' whereabouts.

a mobile is switched on, it transmits a signal to passing beacons, even when it is not being used. This is known as a recognition call and allows the beacon to pick up and send messages if the mobile is used.

The police have enormous powers to snoop on citizens. Police forces in Britain can now authorise themselves to trespass on private property in order to place listening devices wherever they like, without needing the consent of a judge or magistrate. The legal test that must be passed by chief constables is subjective: the police must "think it necessary" to place their bugs. These new police powers would also enable them to gather intelligence by snooping around the premises to be bugged, reading correspondence, and copying documents, according to a letter to the press from John Wadham, the director of Liberty, based at 21, Tabard Street, London, SE1. He concluded: "The complaints mechanism proposed . . . will be as ineffective as those for telephone tapping and surveillance by the secret services, which have never yet upheld one single complaint."

Surveillance by government is at the heart of our entire communications system. There is already a massive international network of electronic eavesdropping that listens in to every phone call, every message between computers, every fax. Here we are not talking about little men with headphones. The government's silicon spies are already snooping on PC users in their own homes and a planned spy centre at which police and intelligence officers can eavesdrop on e-mails and internet messages has won £25 million of British government funding. According to a report in the c-Mail section of the *Daily Mail*, they will be able to decode encrypted messages and monitor mobile phone networks. Said the *Mail* report: "Though ministers insist the project is vital to combat increasingly sophisticated computer criminals, there is concern the security services could use the new centre to monitor perfectly innocent people. Already, the mere fact that you use the internet means your lifestyle is on record on computer. In fact, soon it will know more about you than your closest friends or relatives."

This is a reference to "cookies," electronic tracking devices used by millions of sites. They attach themselves to the hard disc of your computer and send back information to the firm which planted the cookie. Building up a profile of your interests is the name of the game. The ease with which this incredibly detailed information can be gathered—and is being gathered—shocks those who find out about it for the first time. The net is inherently insecure and other machines look at what is on your PC ten, twenty, or even thirty times a day, according to computer expert Jim Gilligan of the University of the West of England. There are defences against this electronic tracking. For example, free software called firewalls is available which stops information being sent to other computers without the user's permission. Most of us are unlikely to bother with this—leaving us wide open to the invisible spies. I have a firewall and it regularly flashes up information that someone is trying to penetrate my computer files.

You might imagine that there is so much traffic over the internet that your few messages are long lost in the ether. You would be wrong. E-mails and newsgroup postings can be retrieved and read by anyone. They are currently available as far back as 1976. I doubt if Monica Lewinsky ever thought her private e-mails to Linda Tripp would end up on CNN's website! There are websites such as *www.reference.com* and *www.dejanews.com* which keep electronic archives of things written on most newsgroups. E-mail messages seem like they are private, but e-mail programs keep a record of every message sent, while the recipients could also file them or send them on to hundreds of other people. Computers at the NSA in America and GCHQ in Cheltenham, England, currently being rebuilt in one of the biggest projects in Europe, can already search through every word that crosses the Atlantic electronically. Key in "New World Order" and I guarantee you will have their instant attention.

Once my wife Pat was talking to one of her sisters in St. Louis, Missouri, on a transatlantic phone line. She had mentioned the NWO in the course of their chat. They were cut off. Neither had time to do anything before, at both ends, the phones rang. They had been reconnected, without having to dial! As far as I know, that is impossible. It seemed odd at the time. Did someone's tape run out? Or am I being paranoid? I doubt if I will ever know. What I do know is that secret government agencies on both sides of the Atlantic are currently spying on their own law-abiding, patriotic citizens, monitoring their websites, and listening to their phone calls. One person who suffers from this, and has many a tale to tell about odd phone occurrences, says that before you dial, or just before you expect an incoming call, pull the phone plug from the wall and then reattach it. This breaks their connection for long enough. As the current joke goes: just because you're paranoid doesn't meant they aren't after you.

We have a friend who tried to buy a book banned in Britain, called *Antichrist and a Cup of Tea*. After she logged on to an American website promoting the book, all kinds of odd things happened to her computer. Her e-mail number was targeted hundreds of times and repeated attempts were made to hack into her system. Her son happens to be a computer whiz and set about tracking these hits. They all came from what he presumed was a government interception center at Milton Keynes, Buckinghamshire. The family started to fight back, erecting a firewall around their computers and complaining to anyone who would listen of illegal attempts to break into their computer. They had the number of the site from which the hits came and made such a fuss with the authorities that the hits ceased.

Simon Davies, director of Privacy International, says that intelligence agencies have for years been vetting and analysing countless phone calls. In Britain the state can do more or less as it pleases with our data. Further, they make it a widespread practice to allow backdoor access to new technologies, enabling them to access data at will. The existence of something called Echelon has recently become widely known. This is a huge network of spy installations that trawls the global telecommunications system, using super-computers to analyse millions of messages and phone calls for key words. Europe and the USA have been spying together since 1947 when the world was divided into five regions for the purposes of eavesdropping. Simon says that early in 1999 the European Parliament passed laws forcing all telecommunications companies to make their equipment wiretap friendly. He says this has laid the foundations for a huge eavesdropping operation, covering all mobile phones, fax messages, internet communications, and pagers in Europe. This system, called "Enfopol," also has a subject tagging system able to track targets—people like you or I—wherever we travel.

It gets worse. Something called the "International User Requirements for Interception" (IUR) means the tagging system can create a data processing and transmission network that cannot only gather names, addresses, and phone numbers of targets and associates, but e-mail addresses, credit card transaction details, PINS, and passwords. The system can also merge mobile phone data to create a total geographic location tracking system. Simon Davies says that the plan was drawn up in secret by police and justice officials as part of a Europe-wide strategy to spy on people across national boundaries. The FBI has worked with the EU to create a top secret organisation called the International Law Enforcement Telecommunications Seminar. The two systems, one designed for national security and the other for law enforcement, will merge. Simon Davies notes that this process will finally eliminate national control over surveillance activities.

For those familiar with Bible prophecy, all this fits neatly into the picture. When world government comes, it will be the ideal tool to instantly identify and eliminate dissenters—and all their friends and relatives. The Nazis would have loved it.

When the British and Irish governments were trying to trace the bombers who blew apart the centre of Omagh, Northern Ireland, in August 1998, it was clear that detectives had access to everyone's private phone calls, as Royal Ulster Constabulary sources said that five hundred million phone calls were checked during their inquiry. Some British police call the mobile phone "the grass in your pocket." "Grass" is underworld slang for informer. There is a vast listening post at Menwith Hill near Harrogate, Yorkshire, which features twenty-two large white "golf ball" style listening devices, known as radomes. This base works in conjunction with the National Security Agency base at Ford Meade, Maryland, home to some of the world's largest supercomputers which analyse countless billions of items of information, much of them gleaned from intercepted phone calls, fax messages, computer and data transmissions, mobile phone calls, etc. Particular words or voices can be scanned for.

In America alone eighty thousand people work at the National Security Agency, so secret it was once known as "No Such Agency." Among other things, they listen in on what seem like private conversations. Since the 1980s the British and American governments have boosted their worldwide capacity to listen in on your phone calls. They are also working to stop encryption software.

People should wake up and protest this invasion of privacy while there is still time—and while we still have a government which is forced to listen to the people. Once the European superstate takes over more aspects of running the country, such protests will be a waste of time. We must not set a pattern of snooping on one another. If you are thinking about looking into your employees' or colleagues' private electronic files, remember—some government agency may be having similar thoughts about *you!*

Chapter 12

Introducing Antichrist

All true Christians, once they realise that it is biblical, are looking for the return of our Lord. Many are also, as commanded, praying for the peace of Jerusalem. But someone else comes first, someone who causes the chaos that will be resolved by our Lord's return to create the peace of Jerusalem. For peace is the last word that will be associated with the "holy land" in the next few years. As the Jewish-American Bible teacher Jacob Prasch once said—it's about as holy as Aldershot on a Friday night. Aldershot, home of the British Army and with numerous taverns, is a good place to avoid on a Friday night.

Somewhere in the world today is the man who will become Antichrist, emperor and dictator of the world. Jeanne Dixon of Washington, D.C., claims a "new messiah" was born on February 5, 1962, a man born under the sign of Aquarius to lead the world into the Age of Aquarius. At the time, all eight planets were in Aquarius, which had not occurred for around two thousand years. Before dawn on that day Mrs. Dixon allegedly had a vision of a baby born to a pharoah and Queen Nefertiti. The baby grew into a wise man worshipped by people of all races and religions, as recounted in *A Gift of Prophecy: The Phenomenal Jeanne Dixon* by Ruth Montgomery. Beware of false prophets like Dixon, for they can be used to lead the faithful astray, although I personally do not doubt that the man who will become Antichrist *is* living on the earth today. I was born under the sign of Aquarius, but I don't follow the stars. I follow the one who created the stars . . .

"Spot the Antichrist" is a game played by some Christians who are true Bible students, who correctly believe in the pre-millennial Rapture of the church and a seven-year period of great trouble before Christ's return. I have done it, although I should know better. I even worked for a New Age occultist who was a very dominant personality, thought he was one of the end-times great masters and had the number plate 666 on his car, although he told me this was coincidental. We jokingly called him "the beast." I also lived in the town which was the home of the self-styled "Great Beast," black magician Aleister Crowley, who liked to be called "the wickedest man who ever lived." He ended up a pathetic, broken man and his family brewery was turned into a housing estate. The only trace of him now is a road name—"Crowley Drive"—in Alton, Hampshire, England.

When I visited the European Parliament, it was an interesting exercise to check out the talent and see if there was a dominant figure. There was only one at that session of parliament and, interestingly, he sat next to me on the aircraft later. Suffice to say, he wasn't the "man of sin" we are awaiting. Poor old Henry Kissinger has been named by some, and he is certainly one of those paving the way for a one-world system. A misguided, influential man, but no Antichrist. How do I know for sure? Because Antichrist will be of Roman descent and Henry is Jewish, a refugee from Hitler's Holocaust.

Other people point to Prince Charles, but I think not. Antichrist will be dominant and intelligent. Charles is indecisive and wimpish. I spoke at the East Coast Prophecy Conference of Southwest Radio Church Ministries, in Willow Valley, Pennsylvania, on the theme of the European Union and the coming Antichrist. Afterward I was approached by a man who had worked out exactly who Antichrist was, his name (which conveniently added up to 666), his age, and the exact number of years before he took power. This was well over twenty, as this personage was but a toddler at present. I didn't argue, as when people have fixed notions there is little point. However, we needn't bother with "spot the antichrist" games. Our job is to tell people the truth until it is no longer possible.

The world is unlikely to know for sure who Antichrist is until the leader steps forward to sign a seven-year peace treaty with Israel, almost certainly on behalf of the European Union. This will be the man of sin, and the numeric value of his name will be 666. By then I don't expect to be around, and those of you who aren't Christians, but are reading this book for fun, would be wise to give your lives to the Lord immediately so you escape the wrath to come. Jesus declared that at the time of His second coming the mood and manners of earth will be as they were in the days of Noah. Then there was apostasy on earth, people were spiritual, acknowledging a supreme being, but they were not godly. Today all the talk is of a God of love, which He is, but there is no mention of a God of judgment, a holy God who hates sin.

The original plans of God for marriage and the unique roles of men and women were being disregarded in the days of Noah, and today as I write there is talk of homosexual marriages in Britain, as there already are in Vermont, USA. Now things are going one step further, with the news that it may soon be possible for two men to have a baby together, using modified sperm in some hellish, unnatural way. Gene scientists, who first cloned sheep in Scotland, are now way down the line to cloning people, something I am certain God will not allow to happen, as He is the only creator.

Women, too, are often no longer content to acknowledge male leadership. The result is the weird sight of women trying to prove that they can do anything men can do. That they manifestly can't is obvious to anyone who sees the female soldiers slogging round the assault courses of Aldershot, the garrison town in which I work. However hard they puff and perspire, they just can't hack it. Their bodies are not made for heavy duty punishment, for carrying assault rifles and learning to bayonet people. Many women have also come to grief trying to emulate male firefighters. God gave men and women different, complimentary gifts. Women are good at serving and caring tasks; men who do these jobs are frequently homosexual. We should all have servant spirits, however, and not be too proud to carry out menial tasks for one another or our bosses. This applies to both sexes.

In the days of Noah "the sons of God saw the daughters of men that they were fair; and they took them wives of all which they chose." In the Old Testament, "sons of God" means angels. These were angels who fell with Lucifer, were thrown out of heaven and decided to marry mortal women. The Old Testament calls them Nephilim, which means "fallen ones." The result of the union of angels and women was a race of giants. These were the beings God wiped out by the flood. Now, at the end of history, we are seeing a repeat performance. There is again association between women—witches—and fallen angels. This is known today in occult circles. From one such association, between Satan himself and an Italian woman, Antichrist will arise—almost certainly has already arisen—and is just awaiting his moment to stride on to the stage of history.

Judas Iscariot was said by Jesus to be a demon—a fallen angel sent to frustrate God's plan of redemption. "Have not I chosen you twelve, and one of you is a devil [a demon]" (John 6:70)—he spoke of Judas Iscariot. Again, "Those that thou gavest me I have kept, and none of them is lost, but the son of perdition" (John 17:12). When another apostle was being chosen in place of Judas, Peter says: "Judas, by transgression, fell, that he might go to his own place" (Acts 1:25). Jesus knew from the beginning exactly what Judas was. John 6:64 says: "For Jesus knew from the beginning who they were that believed not, and who should betray him." He also said that Judas "is" a demon, not that he had one. The "place" that Judas went to was probably Tartarus, the place of imprisoned demons. The "Man of Sin," "the Antichrist" may well eventually be possessed by the demon who inhabited Judas Iscariot. A man cannot be reincarnated, but a demon can take on another body.

This will be the body of a striking young man of fierce countenance, not a portly, middle-aged politician, but someone in the mould of the young Kennedys—and with the same morals. Like Adolph Hitler, who was a type of antichrist and the last man to try to unite Europe under one government, this leader will have a mesmeric personality, a bewitching way of speaking, and the power to command great crowds of followers. "All the world will wonder after him," such will be his magnetism. At present he is restrained by the true church, but once the church is removed he will take his place. Few preachers will understand enough to realise what is going on or challenge it. Many have long ceased to believe in the supernatural, if they ever did. Those who do enjoy supernatural manifestations have no discernment and think all signs and wonders are from God. There are scores of examples of this in disgraceful pseudo-Christian nonsense like the goings on at the Toronto Airport Church, home of the so-called laughing revival, and the fiascos at Brownsville, Texas, and Pensacola, Florida.

Even fewer politicians will challenge Antichrist; these are old, tired men with no charisma, as anyone who ever attends political meetings understands at once. It is not difficult to dominate in their company, for few of the finest, noblest minds go into politics today. I can imagine Lucien, or whatever Antichrist is called, striding into the assembly of the European Union. A tall, dominating figure with great intellect, arresting looks, commanding manner, and air of authority; a hush would fall as all eyes followed him to the rostrum. There he would speak cleverly, clearly, charismatically, and soon he would have this parade of second-raters doing whatever he wanted. They can seldom agree on anything, have no clear ideas of their own and have already cried out for a strong leader. This they will get. But they won't enjoy it very much.

Over three and a half years Antichrist will extend his hold over earth. Media and communications will come under his direct control. I find it particularly interesting that many of the mega-mergers going on in big business involve telecommunications, broadcasting, and food production. Already there are just two cable telecom firms left in Britain and there is a suggestion that they should merge. I knew the head of one of these firms as they were getting established in Britain and asked him how easy it would be to monitor conversations. "Very easy," he replied. "But why would I want to, Alan?" I have no doubt he would not.

The technology that enables increased electronic surveillance into every home is getting smarter all the time. For example, when I decided to take Sky Television's new digital satellite service (Fox Network in the USA) I had to sign an agreement that my family's

TV viewing would be monitored. A cable was installed linking our satellite hook-up with our telephone line. Every day, details of our viewing go to a central computer aimed at building a pattern of what we like to watch. Now the purpose, as far as I know, is purely commercial. But it is just another link in the electronic chain with which we are being bound, all ready for the ultimate control-freak.

For within a year or two of the signing of the treaty with Israel, Antichrist will have total control of the world. Nobody will be able to buy or sell unless they have, on their forehead or right hand, the computer mark of the beast, almost certainly a tiny microchip.

I have spoken to the first man in the world to have a computer chip inserted under his skin, Professor Kevin Warwick of Reading University in Berkshire. Kevin used a tiny six dollar chip for his experiment, during which he opened doors, turned on his office computer, and adjusted his central heating system without lifting a finger. Professor Warwick, head of cybernetics at Reading University, was the first human guinea pig to have an under-the-skin "smart card." He appeared on

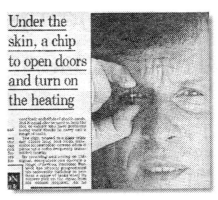

Professor Kevin Warwick of Reading University, England—the first man in the world to have a chip implanted under his skin to perform pre-programmed tasks like opening his office door and turning on his computer.

TV with "X-Files" actress Gillian Anderson who called him "Britain's leading prophet of the robot age." Newspapers were full of the wonders of Kevin's experiment, majoring on the good news that we will soon be able to throw away our plastic credit cards. Cards can be lost, stolen, copied, or damaged. They are a constant headache. We lose them, we worry about them. You can see how easy it will be to persuade an unthinking population how superior a chip implant will be. You can't steal an implant, unless you chop someone's hand or head off! The latter is what will happen to those who refuse the mark—the Tribulation saints.

Kevin Warwick told the press:

With the implant in me it creates a high-speed link from my body and my unique identity to a range of computers. It is already far quicker than using a conventional smart card for these basic operations. This is just the beginning of how this could work. The potential of this technology is enormous. We will be able to communicate directly with computers. For example, it is quite possible for an implant to replace an Access, Visa, or bankers' card. There is very little danger in losing an implant or having it stolen. An implant could also carry huge amounts of data such as National Insurance number and blood types.

But Kevin, who is not part of some evil conspiracy, but a dedicated scientist with a good mind, gave a warning:

I know all this smacks of Big Brother. With an implant a machine will know where anyone is at all times. Individuals could be clocked in and out of their offices automatically. It would be known at all times exactly where an individual was within a building and whom they were with. An individual might not even be able to pay a visit to the toilet without a machine knowing about it.

In fact this is already happening. I know of companies where every employee has swipe cards with them at all times, to gain access to different areas of their headquarters building. A log is kept of their movements. It is already possible to track every keystroke on a computer and relay the findings to the boss's room. Because of this device, costing only ninety-nine dollars, several Americans have already lost their jobs.

Professor Warwick's secretary said that one advantage of his chip implant was that she could trace him at all times. "Since the implant we always know where he is," she said. Professor Warwick advocates that students should be fitted with chips to check their attendance at lectures. "It is a desirable technical advance but we have to decide on the moral and ethical issues of 24-hour surveillance of everyone fitted with a chip," he said. He believes the ultimate application will be to tap into the brain's thought processes, currently a mystery to scientists.

The professor seems to think that man is in charge of his destiny, which is an ever onward, ever upward forward progression. Yet progress is only possible within the rule of law. In much of the West today, the spirit of lawlessness grows fiercer as Antichrist's time draws near. In turn-of-the-century Britain, up to three–quarters of the children were in Sunday schools on the Sabbath. The population may not have all been Christian, but by and large Christian influences prevailed. People knew right from wrong. If you went to a football match, people behaved themselves. Today lawlessness and lewd behaviour rules the streets, even in quiet, British market towns in the country. The very existence of right and wrong is constantly questioned. "This is my right—you can have your own." It's a sort of do-it-yourself morality. Very few children go to Sunday school now, a relative handful in even large churches. They have no grounding in right or wrong, no knowledge of Jesus. Each generation grows up more lawless than the last, something which is obvious to those of us who have seen the generations since the war.

The arts in particular have been degraded and if you go to an art gallery today you may see a pile of dung, a heap of rubbish, or an unmade bed. "Who are we to judge—it's all relative." A music teacher, a man educated enough to know better, recently introduced his class to a series of strange disconnected sounds. Today's new music. Anything goes. Two trash cans banging together is as good as Mozart. Or so some would have you believe . . .

We who use the Bible as our measure of holiness, our means of discernment, will soon be in for some tough times when our faith is put to the test. All this is being foreshadowed in the world's news media every day, for those with eyes to see.

Speaking of music, too many churches become pale parodies of rock concert halls when charismania sweeps in. Hey, man, it's "performance church." Loud rock music is heard in many Sunday services, with the beat encouraging people to get up, fling themselves about, and lose their inhibitions. In fact, having inhibitions, not wanting to leap about wildly, was almost a sin in one big charismatic church we used to attend, where people were encouraged

to get up and start bopping—and if they did not they were accused
of having hang-ups. I remember one Sunday when I refused to
take my shoes and socks off. Those of us who stayed shod were
roundly condemned as not being in the new move of the spirit, or
of quenching the spirit. Some spirits—not the Holy Spirit—need
quenching, but the ministers of this church didn't seem to understand that. Like many others, we had become enmeshed in the charismatic movement. Needless to say, we left that church many years
ago.

We are told to come out of the world, not to conform to it.
When the church tries to ape the world, it usually makes itself look
foolish, like the middle-aged vicar joining in the youth club rock
dance. When I was a young Christian my wife and I took my mother
along to a so-called Christian outreach at Guildford Civic Hall in
the county of Surrey. I was astounded to see a full rock group line
up on stage, complete with massive sound system. Oddly enough, I
had once been in a successful Guildford-based rock group, billed
as "Surrey's top group," although I doubt that we were. Anyway,
the scene of many a Primevals' (that was us) triumph was Guildford
Civic Hall. I had played the drums on stage there scores of times,
at New Year's Eve dances and so forth. So the setting was familiar
to me. So were the sounds, when the group started up. It was just
like any other rave night at the Civic, with lots of noise, teenage
couples lying together on the floor and shouting out to each other,
and a general air of raucous licentiousness. Fortunately the sound
level was so shattering, and we were in the front row, that I don't
really think mother ever quite realised what was going on. She
certainly wasn't saved. Who could have been? This is not the way
the world will ever turn to Christ.

While some services have become very sensual, others are just
plain short; a quick hymn sandwich, a prayer, the notices, a little
homily about doing good, and they're quickly off for tea, coffee
and cookies. I live near one denominational church where they are
in and out within the hour on Sundays, taught, if that is the word,
by a woman minister. In the foyer of the church hall was a poster
for a yoga class. This is not a church that can withstand false teach-

ing, let alone the power of Antichrist with his lying signs and wonders.

Another church in Britain has christened the babies of two homosexual men, who paid an American woman to conceive for them. With the legalisation of homosexual marriages a coming certainty in Britain—stopping it would be illegal because it would be classed as "discriminatory"—I predict the first homosexual marriage in church within a short time. This is *with* the true Christians on the earth. Just imagine how foul, how violent, how unsafe the world will be when we are gone.

This is the time when the Beast will make war on the saints, those people saved during the Tribulation. He will overcome them and will wield authority over every tribe and people, tongue and nation on earth. This man, the personification of evil, will rule over ten regions, whose leaders or "kings" unite to give him leadership. Their people "believe the lie," for reasons I have partly detailed above. The confederacy of nations Antichrist will rule over has come about abruptly, since the Second World War. Antichrist will rule over this federation for seven years, using it as his base to run the world. Most people will follow him, believing the strong delusion of 2 Thessalonians 2:12. They will be used of him until he has no further need of them, just as the great whore church will be destroyed in a day on the hills of Rome, around the mid-way point of the Tribulation, after three and a half years. Rome doubly deserves judgment, by the way, as it now seems that the Colosseum, where so many saints were martyred, was built on the proceeds of spoils of war taken from the Temple in Jerusalem after Roman soldiers sacked the building in A.D. 70—two years before work began on the Colosseum.

Following the destruction of Rome, Antichrist will rule on his own, empowered by Satan, on a three and a half year mission of destruction, with the main focus on the Jews and any saved Christians. Even his image will have the power to cause death to those who defy him—and it will be set up in the Temple in Jerusalem, which will shortly be rebuilt, according to prophecy. Already the Temple vessels have been cast and are on show in an exhibition in

Jerusalem. Young men from the tribe of Levi have been trained as
Temple priests, a nearly perfect red heiffer has been bred for the
sacrifices to restart, and all that remains is for the actual structure
to go up, alongside the Dome of the Rock, where there is ample
room. When a friend of mine asked the Jews in charge if they already had the stones cut for the Temple, he was told: "Look around
you. We won't be short of rocks for building with." Jerusalem is a
very rocky place. Now that, at the time of writing, Ariel Sharon is
in power, it will be the scene of a few more rocky confrontations,
with Arabs using his leadership as an excuse for violence, as they
did following his earlier trip to the Temple Mount.

This Temple is mentioned in Daniel 12:11, Matthew 14, 2 Thessalonians 11:14, and Revelation 11:1, and it is mentioned in connection with judgment. The first verse of Revelation 11 has it measured with a reed like a rod, the symbol of judgment. Daniel 12:11
speaks of the Abomination of Desolation defiling the Temple, which
will be destroyed. For Antichrist, who initially poses as friend and
protector of the Jews, is really their deadliest enemy who, according to Daniel 9:27 will confirm his covenant with the Jews for one
week, a week of years, but at the end of three and a half years will
cause the sacrifice to cease and he himself to be worshipped. When
the godly Jews refuse to worship the Beast's image, and realise he
has duped them, this is the time they will have to flee or be killed.
"Then let them which be in Judæa flee into the mountains . . . but
pray that your flight be not in the winter, neither on the Sabbath
day" (Matt. 24:16–20). Both halves of the seven-year Tribulation
will contain terrible judgments and disasters, according to Matthew 24:21. However, the greater divine judgments will be in the
last three and a half year period as God pours out his wrath on an
unbelieving, sin-filled world. Many believers who come to faith
during this time will be killed. These are the ones known as the
"Tribulation saints." Most people, including those in the apostate
world church of that time, will see Antichrist's lying signs and
wonders—and will gladly worship him.

The Jews think the Temple they will shortly rebuild is Ezekiel's
Temple, but this is the Temple for the Millennium, the time of Christ's

thousand-year reign on earth, from Jerusalem. This beautiful structure, so minutely described in the Bible, will be erected after peace comes to Israel, after the last of Christ's enemies is vanquished by His return at the head of the hosts of heaven and His saints—the true believers. Shortly after this, Satan, Antichrist, and the False Prophet will be cast into the abyss and all resistance to Jesus will cease.

Non-Christians who hear all this often ask: "Why would a loving God allow the suffering coming during the Great Tribulation?" Well, God is a holy as well as a loving God and the wicked must be judged. Earth has gotten to the state where a holy God can no longer tolerate the sin that abounds across it, the rampant sexual immorality and vileness of abortion. Enough is enough. Also, when it becomes obvious to even the dimmest that God really is judging the earth, as hailstones rain down, volcanoes erupt, and a comet strikes the planet, many millions will at last turn to Him for salvation. In particular, the Jews have to be brought to the point where they can accept God's offer of salvation, rejected two thousand years before when they crucified Jesus.

God will allow Israel's enemies to surround and destroy it, saving only a one-third remnant of the people of Israel. These Jews will shelter in Petra, Jordan, during the last three and a half years of the Tribulation period, being taught by God. Outside in the world will be unprecedented troubles. For details turn to Matthew 24:21–22. In three series of judgments, as shown in Revelation 6:9–16, about three-quarters of the people living on earth will be killed, while earth is made a wasteland. At the time of our Lord's return in triumph with His armies of saints, to do battle with the Antichrist and his armies outside Jerusalem, He will arrive not a minute too soon. For, the Bible tells us, if He waited any longer no life would be left on earth.

After this comes earth's golden thousand years, the time when Christ rules His millennial kingdom from Jerusalem. This will be a time of righteous judgment and the absence of all the things caused by the curse of sin, like sickness and disease. Few people will face death and there will be fullness of joy and a full knowledge of the

Lord (Jeremiah 31:34; Joel 2:28–32.) His kingdom will endure forever (Isaiah 9:6–7), starting with the thousand years at the end of
which Satan will be released to create the last great rebellion on
earth. Following this a new heaven and a new earth will be created
and this is where the eternal kingdom will be situated. It is there
that all Christ's disciples from throughout the ages will reign with
Him.

Chapter 13

The Great Commission

by Pat Franklin

Pat Franklin is an American who came to live in Britain in 1967. She was one of five children in a Catholic family in a suburb of St. Louis, Missouri. She was educated at St. Andrew's School, Bishop Dubourg (Roman Catholic) High School, Harris Teachers' College, and the University of Missouri at St. Louis. After graduation in 1967, she went to live in England, where she works as a journalist. She and her British husband, Alan, have two children. Pat and her three sisters all became born-again believers in the 1980s. Two of the sisters attend evangelical churches and two are at independent Christian fellowships.

In this book my husband Alan has set out what we believe Scripture teaches about the time of the end. As journalists we stand amazed as we begin to see the unfolding of the most sensational events in all of human history. We are even more amazed that the God of history has allowed sinners like us to become his children.

Just to recap, here are the main points:

- Christians have an increasingly hard time as the end approaches, since the world hates us, just as Jesus said it would.
- The struggles we face each day cause us to begin to look up and long for our Savior's return, that He might come and take us to be with Him.
- Immense changes roll through our societies, whatever government is in power.

- Suddenly the Lord Jesus Christ comes in the air with a shout and His sheep hear His voice. Hallelujah! Our troubles are over in a flash and we join the Lord in the air, to be forever with our Savior. Our trials are not worthy to compare with the glory He will reveal to us.

- Our struggles are as nothing compared with the rewards He will give those who have been faithful even in little things. Our pain and sorrow at our own sinfulness is over forever as our Father wipes away every tear. The hard times are gone like a bad dream and at the Lord's right hand there are pleasures forevermore. All loneliness is past, as we join the great family reunion of God, meeting our brothers and sisters from down the centuries, for everyone who loves the Lord will love one another.

- On earth events coalesce into a one-world government (led by the Antichrist) and a one-world church (probably led by the pope of the day). A single currency is used throughout the world and everything is standardised, giving the government total control over people.

- There is nuclear war in the Middle East. Damascus is destroyed during the night. Egypt is a wasteland for forty years. Part of Jordan is a wasteland forever.

- At some stage before the seven-year Tribulation, a confederation led by Russia attacks Israel, but God saves His ancient people (Ezekiel 38 and 39).

- Antichrist rules the world for at least seven years, signing the seven-year peace treaty with Israel, bringing a false peace on earth.

- There are wars, famines, plagues, earthquakes, and even worse to follow.

- Antichrist breaks the treaty in the middle of the seven years and the Jews, most of whom are completely non-religious, flee to Petra (also called Bozrah), a mountain city in Jordan, where they hide and begin to turn back to God.

- The "mark" computer identification system is brought in and everyone must take the mark of the Beast in his right hand or forehead. Without it he cannot buy or sell.

- God's patience is at an end and the day of mercy is over. The world reels under the horrific punishments He rains down on people who have rejected the Lord Jesus and continually refused His mercy and grace. All those who have considered God harsh and blamed Him for all the evils of the world will find to their cost that God now acts in the character they have ascribed to Him. He will indeed allow great catastrophes to come upon them and their children.

- Even the heavenly bodies will be shaken and the earth itself will sway on its axis.

- Armageddon. Antichrist orders all the nations to gather against Jerusalem, because he recognizes that the Lord Jesus is going to come back there.

- The Lord Jesus comes back to earth, first to the Jews at Petra, Jordan, and all Israel is converted as the Jews see at last that Jesus really is their Messiah, the one who was pierced for their transgressions, the Passover Lamb who was slain for their sins, and they mourn as for an only son. The nation is converted in one day. Hallelujah! The Jews, God's ancient people, at long last become our beloved brothers and sisters in Christ.

- The Holy One of Israel leads the armies of heaven against the forces of Antichrist, but the Lord's loved ones have no fighting to do at all—we just shout His praises. To the dismay of the enemy, the Antichrist and False Prophet are taken and thrown into the lake of fire and can do nothing whatever about it. The Lord Jesus destroys all His enemies by the brightness of His coming and the sword of the spirit; the very words of His mouth defeat His foes.

- With His enemies vanquished, there are a short few months while the Lord Jesus rearranges things to His liking.

- Sing hallelujah, for the Lord God Almighty reigns. Our blessed Savior begins His glorious millennial reign, the thousand-year period when the government will at long last be upon His wonderful shoulder.

- Satan is bound in the abyss, a literal place, for one thousand years. We then see what this world could have been like if people had only obeyed God and walked in His ways.
- The Lord Jesus rules this earth with a rod of iron from His capital city of Jerusalem.
- Syria, Israel, and Egypt are united in worshipping the Lord Jesus and the former enemies become like three beloved sisters.
- Those in the Tribulation who resisted Antichrist and tried to help the Jews are allowed to remain on earth during the thousand-year period.
- Israel is the pre-eminent nation on earth and everyone wants to be friends with the Jews.
- The Christians who have returned with the Lord are given authority to rule with Him as He sees fit.
- Rewards for service are handed out. Those who have given up anything for Christ's sake get a hundredfold back. This does not include all those who are giving "seed faith" money in the hopes of getting rich now—they are giving for selfish motives. One man who sold his house and business and gave the cash to an American money preacher is now living in bitter poverty. He was hoping for a hundredfold return now, because he believed the false prophets on religious TV. God does provide for His children in this age, but the mega rewards come in the millennium and the Lord certainly does not want His children giving out of their greed to get lots more money back. We must give out of a pure heart of love for Christ and compassion for people, not greed for more money.
- All nature is changed back to its original state, and the wolf and the lamb can lie down together. Carnivores become herbivores.
- No more war for a thousand years. Praise God.
- The nations send delegates each year to Jerusalem to keep the Feast of Tabernacles. If they do not do this, no rain falls on their countries, so they all make sure to circle the date on

their calendars.

- The earth is filled with the knowledge of God as the waters cover the sea, but, incredibly, the heart of man is still evil and despite all that God has done and that Christ is reigning now on a beautiful, peaceful earth, most of the natural people born during the thousand years do not love the Lord Jesus and they would rather get rid of Him.

- At the end of the thousand years Satan is loosed from the abyss and the people of earth choose to follow him and stupidly believe that they can defeat the Lord Jesus.

- They gather for war and are totally destroyed.

- Satan joins the Antichrist and the False Prophet, who have had the lake of fire all to themselves for a thousand years.

- All unbelievers from all ages are judged at the Great White Throne. Everyone at this judgment is damned. Many of them will be religious people who have followed false religions, hoping their good deeds, church membership, or receiving "the sacraments" will get them to heaven. The Freemasons will be well represented. Some of them are buried with a white lambskin and told that they will wear it at the Great White Throne and that when God sees the lambskin He will let them into heaven. Wrong. If only they would read the Bible and see that only faith in Christ, not membership of a secret organization, is the ticket to heaven. If only they would read Revelation 20 and see that only the damned are judged at the Great White Throne, those who refused to accept Christ as their Savior, those who put their faith in anything other than the Lord Jesus. Those, for example, who put their faith in a lambskin instead of in the holy Lamb of God. I am sorry to say that many Catholics will also be there, because they put their trust in church rituals, instead of believing the Bible and putting all their trust in the Lord Jesus. This may sound like hair-splitting, but it is not. If only they would study the Bible they could come to a living faith in the Savior instead of faith in an organization!

- With all unbelievers dealt with forever, and only Christ's people left, the eternal ages begin.

- The new Jerusalem, the city of God, descends out of heaven to the earth in unimaginable glory and splendor.
- Eye has not seen nor ear heard what God has in store for those who love Him and here we must leave it because we cannot even begin to comprehend the next part.

I hope this is helpful. There is appalling ignorance of these things, because the churches simply do not teach what the Bible says about the future. Back in third grade I asked a nun at our Catholic school about the Book of Revelation. Goodness knows where I had even heard of it, because, like every other Catholic family I knew, we did not own a Bible. The nun told me that all the things in Revelation had already happened long ago. I felt so let down and disappointed.

Many years later we asked a Baptist pastor in Britain about Bible prophecy and the reply was that he had been turned off it by someone he knew who went overboard on the subject. Also, he said he just did not have the time to study it properly and so would not venture to teach on it. What a great pity, because he is a man who loves the Lord very much and we love him. So even his church of born-again believers is largely in ignorance of things the Lord clearly wants us to know.

A Baptist elder told us he believed Genesis literally, but could not accept that the Book of Revelation was also literal.

Most churches in England do not even teach that you need to be born again, so Bible prophecy is way out in the stratosphere as far as they are concerned. One young friend from a Church of England (Anglican) church came with us to a service at an evangelical church to hear a talk about the second coming. She had never heard of the Rapture and she was about to become a full time Church of England youth worker. Her eyes were opened that night, praise the Lord, as a learned man from one of the Brethren assemblies gave an overview of what the Bible teaches is yet to come in human history. The meeting that night was like a light flickering in the sea of darkness covering Britain, but how comforting to warm ourselves in that light!

So, books like this one are obviously still needed and if the ministers and full time religious leaders will not research and write them, it falls to ordinary people like us to attempt the job as best we can. I write this with a sense of trembling, knowing my total unfitness, but also knowing that I have a commission.

Please feel free to copy this chapter and give it to anyone who will read it. The book is obviously copyrighted, but please use my chapter in any way you can think of to get this message out to people, saved and unsaved, that they might know the truth, for only the truth sets us free.

If anyone reading this has now realized that they are not saved and are following some false, deceptive path, now is the time for you to get right with God. Do not leave it or allow yourself to be distracted or sidetracked.

In my own case I came to faith in Christ at the age of thirty-six, and no one could have been more surprised by this than I was. As an American "cradle Catholic," I had totally lost my faith at the age of nineteen during my first year at Harris Teachers' College in St. Louis. After that I never lost a chance to speak out against what I saw as "medieval morality" and hypocrisy. At that time I equated Catholicism with Christianity.

Like most Catholic families, we did not own a Bible. How I wish now that I had read the Bible when I was young and acquired a real faith. How much misery I would have been spared! I "did my own thing." Now I want to do God's thing, not my thing. I will usually get it wrong, but God is never wrong and His ways are best. Like Frank Sinatra, "I did it my way." I wish I hadn't. I'll bet old Frank does too, but it's too late for him. There are no more chances once you are dead.

Despite doing it my way, God had mercy on me. I was like the prodigal, that stupid young person whose only good point was that he had a wonderful father watching for any sign of repentance and for him to come home! Although I did not acknowledge God's existence, my heavenly Father was patiently waiting for me. Years went by until, at the age of thirty-six, as a liberal American agnostic, I ended up in England, married to my British husband, Alan.

The turning point for me came when our son Daniel was three years old. I signed him up for the best playgroup in Alton, Hampshire, where we then lived and it just happened to be run by Alton Evangelical Free Church.

Soon after getting involved with the playgroup, I received a strange letter from my younger sister Carol in October 1980. There were pages and pages of excited writing telling me how she had been "born again." Alan and I thought she had been got at by some weird cult and that we would have to go over to the USA and bring her to her senses.

A few days later I took Daniel to the playgroup. For the first time since we had joined, the pastor of the church visited the group, and went round talking to each of the mothers there. Unknown to me, he had prayed earnestly the night before that God would show him someone whose heart was ready to receive the Lord Jesus and that God would cause that person to use the words "born again" so that he would know who to pray for.

He made the rounds, speaking to all the mothers in the church hall. When he got to me, I was thinking of my sister's letter, and asked him: "Is yours one of these churches that believe in being born again?" Though he did not let on at the time, he knew I was the one he was supposed to pray for. Our conversation lasted just a few minutes. I said something like, "Isn't the Bible just a book of myths and history and poetry?" He gave me a reasoned, but short answer. I also told him I was "beyond the pale" because I was married to a divorced man and so could never be a Christian, which is what I had learned in the Catholic church.

In my years of being far from God I had often said in my arrogance: "I've never met an intelligent Christian." That day I left the playgroup, thinking, "Well, he is really quite intelligent. Hmmm."

That was in October. I continued to see women from the church at the playgroup, but no one tried to get me to go to church. How many of those wonderful women were praying for me, I don't know, but I thank them now with all my heart. I remember thinking then that they were rather odd, because I would often be with one or two of them in the kitchen of the church hall making coffee while the others were out with the children. The odd thing about them was that they never gossiped about the other ones. I found this very strange. I had never known women to get together and not gossip about other women! Strangest of all was one woman, Anne Heath, who was a full-time pastoral care worker for the church, working with the women, children, youth, and old people. Never had I met anyone with such peace. How could she be so serene and happy? I could see it was not just an act.

Weeks passed and God turned up the heat in my life. We used to read a daily newspaper called *The Guardian* which confirmed our liberal philosophy. In January of 1981 it happened to carry a series of articles about a young woman who died of cancer after discovering a black spot on her body. I was avidly following this series, when to my horror, one day in the shower I noticed a black spot on my body. Full of fear, I immediately prayed to the God I did not acknowledge, saying: "If you will let this not be cancer, I will make one last effort to find out if you exist."

I went to see my doctor, who said she thought it was okay, but would send me to a specialist in Winchester to make sure. The day came and the specialist took one look at the spot and said: "You've got nothing to worry about. This is a genetic wart, programmed in your genes to emerge at a precise year, month, and day. Any time you have half an hour free, make an appointment and we can get rid of it for you."

I was walking on air as I left his office. Then I remembered my deal with God and told Him in my mind that I would keep my side of the bargain by reading all of the New Testament, which I had never done before.

Since I was there in Winchester, a beautiful city, I decided to visit the cathedral where I had been a few times before as a tourist, but never a worshipper. With our son Daniel, then three, I went into the ancient stone building and, instead of walking around looking at the architecture, I decided to sit on one of the chairs. The chair in front of me had a rack full of books and I picked one out and opened it.

As I read the words, it was as though they came straight through the roof of Winchester Cathedral and into my head. The words were: "Except a man be born again, he cannot see the kingdom of God" (John 3:3).

I sat there stunned, but somehow knowing that there was something else to come. I read on and, about a page later, came upon these words: "Go ye therefore; and teach all nations, baptizing them in the name of the Father, and of the Son, and of the Holy Ghost: Teaching them to observe all things whatsoever I have commanded you" (Matthew 28:19–20). Once again, the words seemed to come straight through the high roof of the cathedral and into my head.

Tourists were strolling casually around the cathedral and no one had noticed a thing, but I sat there knowing that almighty God had just spoken to me—twice. Suddenly I was not an agnostic any longer. I knew there was a God and that He had communicated with me and it thrilled me to the very depths of my soul.

I thought I understood the second thing he said—that I was to go and tell people something, but what? I had no idea. The first thing, about being "born again" was a total mystery to me. It was under the chapter heading of "Baptism" in the book, but I had already been baptized as a baby, so how could that apply to me? My sister Carol had written about it, but I had not understood a word.

We went home and that night I put Daniel to bed as usual at eight p.m. Alan was working in his office upstairs and I got ready to keep my bargain with God. I went to the bookshelves and got the old King James Bible which Alan was given at the end of secondary school. No one had ever read it and it smelled a little musty. I sat down by the fireplace and opened to the gospel of Matthew and began to read the genealogy of the Lord Jesus Christ.

As soon as I began to read I knew absolutely that every word was true, every line was important and that this book was like no other book on earth, that this was God's book, the book that told the truth about everything. I read for one hour. The next night I did the same thing—put Daniel to bed, came downstairs, read the Bible for one hour.

About ten days later I had gotten to the middle of the gospel of Luke. By then I was so scared and so full of the most dreadful sorrow and remorse, that I did not know what to do. I realized that Jesus was indeed the holy Son of God, so pure and marvelous that I was not worthy to clean His shoes.

I knew that the miracles, which I had previously tried to explain away, were all true. I knew Jesus' teaching on heaven and hell was true and that I was headed straight for hell, and richly deserved to go there. I was thrilled, but sickened by all I read, because I could see that I had got it completely wrong in my life, doing things He said not to do and failing to do things I should have done. I had no faith that anything could be done about this, because I could see I had blown it, and yet through reading the gospels I had gotten to know Jesus and I now loved Him with all my heart.

After the reading one night, in an agony of mind at how I had utterly missed out, I went up to our bedroom and got down on my knees. It was almost like there were invisible bees buzzing around my head, saying things like: "You're not going to pray, are you—your friends will think you're crazy" and, "You're not going to give Him your life, are you—He might make you give away all your money!" I remember sort of swiping all these thoughts away with my hand, thinking, as far as money was concerned, that Jesus owned the whole world anyway; it was all His already and I could not even take one more breath unless He allowed it.

I then prayed what I now know as "the sinner's prayer." I had never heard of that in the Catholic church. Here is the gist of what I prayed:

Lord Jesus, I see now that every word in Your book is true. You really are who You said You were and You really did all those miracles. You are the Son of God. I have done so many things wrong. I got it completely wrong and committed so many sins. Oh, Lord Jesus, please forgive me. [I thought through my entire life here and brought before Him every single sin I could remember.] I give You everything I have—my house, my money, any time I have left. You can have every minute. Only please forgive me and please, please, let me be one of Your people.

I nearly cried my eyes out, and did not for one minute believe that
He would forgive me, because I thought I was far too bad. And yet,
I continued reading the Bible and a few days later told Anne Heath
at the playgroup what I had prayed. I said I didn't think that the
Lord Jesus would want anything to do with me, as I had really
blown it. Her reply was: "Pat, that was all He was waiting for!"

She made an appointment to meet with me. On that wonderful
day she brought her Bible and showed me a list of scriptures about
salvation like the following:

> If we confess our sins, he is faithful and just to forgive us our
> sins, and to cleanse us from all unrighteousness.
>
> —1 John 1:9

> For God so loved the world, that he gave his only begotten Son,
> that whosoever believeth in him should not perish, but have ever-
> lasting life.
>
> —John 3:16

> . . . if thou shalt confess with thy mouth the Lord Jesus, and shalt
> believe in thine heart that God hath raised him from the dead,
> thou shalt be saved.
>
> —Romans 10:9

> Therefore being justified by faith, we have peace with God through
> our Lord Jesus-Christ. . . .
>
> —Romans 5:1

> There is therefore now no condemnation to them which are in
> Christ Jesus. . . .
>
> —Romans 8:1

> Therefore if any man be in Christ, he is a new creature: old things
> are passed away; behold, all things are become new.
>
> —2 Corinthians 5:17

> For you are all the children of God by faith in Christ Jesus.
>
> —Galatians 3:26

For by grace are ye saved through faith; and that not of your-
selves; it is the gift of God; Not of works, lest any man should
boast. . . .

—Ephesians 2: 8–9

We read them together and, incredibly, I began to realize what had
happened to me. If those scriptures were true, and I knew that
every word in the Bible was true, then it meant unequivically that
God had forgiven me, my sins were wiped away, they were cast as
far as the east is from the west (Psalm 103:12) and I was a new
creation. Old things were passed away and I was born again!

A big smile spread across my face and Anne Heath said that
yes, this is what had happened to me. I think that smile stayed on
my face for about three months. I wanted to rush up to everyone I
saw and ask them if they were saved. I wanted to tell them the
wonderful tidings of salvation, that it was possible for them to have
their sins forgiven, the slate wiped clean, and to be assured—to be
absolutely sure, on God's solid gold guarantee—of a place reserved
for them in heaven.

How I thank God for His great mercy on a sinner like me.

As a Catholic I could never be sure of God's mercy and certainly not of going to heaven. We had to keep going to mass, taking
the sacraments, keeping "holy days of obligation," racking up indulgences to reduce our burning time in "purgatory," but even then
we might do something wrong at the end and be sent to hell. As a
lapsed Catholic turned agnostic, I had chucked the whole lot overboard. Was I a Christian when I was a Catholic girl? No, definitely
not. I was just a churchgoer who was trying to be a good person. I
mentally agreed with church teaching, but it is quite another thing
to have saving faith. Saving faith is simply putting your faith in the
Lord Jesus—and not adding anything to that. Not Jesus plus your
good deeds, not Jesus plus church membership or sacraments or
rosaries— not Jesus plus anything else. Jesus alone can save us.
We can add nothing to what He has accomplished on the cross.
When you do put your faith in Christ alone and ask Him (not some
priest) to forgive you, you will be saved. Then it is as if God turns

the light on inside you, causing you to be born again of the Holy Spirit, making you a new creation spiritually and sealing you with the Holy Spirit so that you can never ever lose your salvation. Before that I was spiritually dead. After my conversion in 1981 my spirit was alive at last and I could begin to understand spiritual things.

At last I knew the truth and the truth had set me free. I had chapter and verse. I knew for sure I was going to heaven. Not because I was good; I was anything but! I knew it was true because God said so in the Bible. It is there in black and white, the very words of God Almighty to all who will turn to Him and put their faith in the Lord Jesus Christ—not in religious observances.

Please, dear reader, do your utmost to come to a saving faith in Jesus Christ. You may think, like me, that you are too bad to become a Christian, but that is just a lie of Satan! Jesus did not come for the righteous, but for sinners! For me! And you too.

On the other hand, you may think you are already good enough. Oh dear, that is another lie of Satan, for no one is good enough. All have sinned and fallen short. All, every single person, including you. Even Mary said she needed a Savior! She said: "My soul doth magnify the Lord, And my spirit hath rejoiced in God my Savior" (Luke 1:46–47).

Actually, most people I have tried to tell about Jesus are in a fool's paradise and think they will be okay. "I've lived a good life," they say, or "I've never done anything too terrible." A surprising number of people say, "I've never robbed a bank." This always amuses me, as if God will say: "Okay, bank robbers to the left. Non-bank robbers to the right. You have managed to live all your lives without robbing a bank, so you can come into heaven." Well, I never robbed a bank either, but I was certainly going to hell. The "good" people worry me; it is hard to make them see the danger they are in or the urgency of seeking God while there is time.

My own daughter Anne was in this category. I used to read the Bible to our two children at bedtime. By the way, this was not a watered down child's version, but my own adult Bible. Though I did paraphrase some scriptures as I read, I knew my children could understand a great deal and it was good for them to hear God's Word. One night in the reading Jesus mentioned hell. Annie, then aged four, piped up: "I know what hell is—that's where the bad people go."

"No," I said, "it is not that simple. Hell is where *everybody* is going, unless they put their trust in the Lord Jesus and ask Him to forgive their sins. It doesn't matter how good they think they are; no one is good enough. It doesn't matter if they helped old ladies across the street or raised a million dollars for charity—nothing they can do is good enough to get them into heaven. They are all going to hell unless they put their faith in Jesus."

Her little eyes opened wide. "You mean *good* people are going to hell?" she asked. I told her: "They only think they're good and maybe other people think they're good too, but the Bible tells us that no one is good but God and they are certainly going to hell unless they believe in the Lord Jesus."

"Well how can you make sure you go to heaven?" she asked. I told her you had to admit that you were a sinner and ask Jesus to forgive you for all the bad things you did or thought. "Well I'm not going to do that!" she declared. You see, she was a sweet little thing and everyone always told her what a good girl she was, so she had no intention of admitting that she had ever thought or done anything wrong.

"Okay, you don't have to do it. Jesus never forced anybody," I told her. "It's entirely up to you." We left it there, but the next day Annie asked me again: "Tell me about those good people that are going to hell." We had the same conversation and again she declared that she did not want to say that prayer.

The next day she asked again and I told her and again she said she didn't want to say those words.

The fourth day happened to be Alan's birthday. Annie was coloring at the kitchen table. I was washing dishes when she looked up and asked: "How did you say you become a Christian?" I told her again. "I can't remember to say all that!" she said. "I could say it a little bit at a time and you could say it after me," I told her. "Okay, go on then," she said, a little bit crossly I might add.

So, still washing dishes, I led her in the sinner's prayer, a bit at a time. At the end she said, "I'm a Christian now," and went straight back to her coloring. I thought, we shall see if you really are, because if Christ comes into someone's heart, there is mega change. They are born again and become a new creation and there is a very big difference, even if you are a "good girl" aged four.

That night after the bedtime Bible reading she asked if she could pray. When she prayed it was always the same: "Dear God, please give me a bear and a horse and a dog and a rabbit (and any other animal that came to mind)." That night it was entirely different. She folded her hands, closed her eyes, and soared off into a prayer of thanks and praise, thanking God for everything she could think of, including trees, bark on trees, butterflies, logs, etc., until the end, "and thank you for the best thing you ever made, the flowers."

My heart was singing as I tucked her in, and for months after that she would spontaneously burst into prayers of thanks and praise. Once I was driving and she was in her child seat in the back when she piped up: "Why don't we just praise the Lord for this lovely day?" "Good idea, Annie, you start," I said. "Oh dear Lord, thank you so much for this beautiful day," she began, as we drove through the grey drizzle. So you see, I knew that the wonderful thing had indeed happened and she was truly born again of the Holy Spirit of God. She was a new creation and her heart was full of praise and love.

She had thought she was good enough, but it was only when she admitted that in fact she wasn't good enough at all that God could come into her heart.

I had thought I was too bad; Annie had thought she was already acceptable to God. We were both wrong. God wanted both of us to come to Him in humility and ask forgiveness and to be made one of His children.

How about you, dear reader? You are not too bad to be saved. Jesus' blood can make the foulest clean! And you are not so good that you do not need forgiveness. It was your sins too which Jesus bore upon the cross.

Can you humble yourself and admit that you too are a sinner

and need God's forgiveness? Sin is not just doing bad things—even thinking hateful thoughts is sin and we cannot help ourselves, as we are born sinners and will die sinners unless we come to real faith in Christ and receive the Holy Spirit. A new life awaits you if you put your faith in the Lord Jesus, a life with unimaginable joy at the end of it. Death will lose its sting and become nothing more than a step into glory.

Only God can forgive you—not some priest in a confessional. The old system of priests and people is gone. Jesus cried: "It is finished!" on the cross, as the veil of the Jewish Temple split from top to bottom. After that anyone could have access to God through faith in Jesus without going through a priest. Anyone who sets himself or herself up as a priest, a mediator between you and almighty God, is totally wrong and completely out of line. God ripped that Temple veil from the top. Now, through faith in the blood of Jesus, we can run straight to Him, right into His throne room, crying, "Father!" No earthly mediator, only Jesus, our High Priest, our Savior. No one "standing in the place of Jesus" as the pope claims to do. That is blasphemous. No one stands in Jesus' shoes! He is all in all and He will not share His glory with another.

Only faith in the Lord Jesus will get you into heaven. Being good won't do it because our good deeds are like filthy rags to God, unless they are done "in Christ"—filtered through Him after we are born again. We just cannot ever be good enough in ourselves; yet in Him we become able to go boldly in prayer to God, knowing that He will hear us if we pray in Jesus' name and according to His will.

It is certainly God's will that you put your faith in the Lord Jesus—the real, historical Jesus, not some counterfeit—and ask for forgiveness and for Him to make you one of His people. God's will can be done in your life today. Don't leave it till another day—there might not be another day for you!

If you do put your faith in the Lord Jesus as your Savior, you are now my beloved brother or sister, whatever your age, your color, your nationality—our Father loves variety! We'll meet one day in our Father's house, and oh how we'll sing His praises together!

Bibliography

I have drawn upon so many sources in writing this book that it is impossible to list them—it would require two chapters of notes!

Sources have included the newspapers and magazines of Britain and America, news services, specialist publications, and internet web sites. A considerable part of the information has been gleaned first hand by myself and my wife, in our jobs as editors and writers for a variety of publications.

Other valuable information has come in Britain from Christian speakers and writers like Tony Pearce, director of the Messianic Testimony and publisher of the Christian newsletter *Light for the Last Days* (Box BM-4226 London, WC1N 3XX); Jacob Prasch, whose excellent books are available via St. Matthew Publishing Ltd. of 24, Geldart Street, Cambridge, CB1 2lX, England, tel 01223 504871; also the source of many other excellent Christian books, and the authoritative Christian magazine *Vanguard* at PO Box LB1475, London, WIA 9LB. I have drawn on anti- EU newsletters like *Facts, Figures and Phantasies* (20 Ramillies Road, London, W4 1JN); *Eurofacts* (PO Box 9984 London W12 8WZ); and *Portman Papers* (20, Portmans, North Curry, Taunton, Somerset, TA3 6NL, UK.) The Conservative Party's website at *www.conservatives.com* is a useful source of information on the emerging EU superstate and the Eurocorps army.

Other book sources include *The Castle of Lies* by Christopher Booker and Richard North—subtitled "Why Britain must get out of Europe," published by Duckworth, 48, Hoxton Square, London, NI 6PB; *The Principality and Power of Europe* by Adrian Hilton,

Dorchester House Publications, Box 67, Rickmansworth, Herts, WD3 5SJ; *New World Order (The Ancient Plan of Secret Societies)* by William T. Still, Huntington House, Inc.; *Big Brother NSA and its "Little Brothers"* by Terry L. Cooke, SCM Publishing, Bend, Oregon; *The Two Babylons* by the Rev. Alexander Hislop, available from B. McCall Barbour of 28, George IV Bridge, Edinburgh, EH1 1ES, Scotland; *Please Tell Me* and *The Deadly Deception*, two highly informed books about Freemasonry by Tom C. McKenney, published by Huntington House Publishers and, of course, *The King James Bible*.

From America we have drawn on the resources of Southwest Radio Church Ministries (PO Box 100, Bethany, OK, 73008) and Hearthstone Publishing (PO Box 815, Oklahoma City, OK 73127), publishers of this and many other books by reputable Christian authors. I recommend their website, *www.swrc.com*

Also Dave Hunt's *Berean Call* of PO Box 7019, Bend, Oregon 97708, website at *www. thebereancall.org*. All Dave Hunt's booklist is recommended and should be in every church library. We commend Dr. Arnold Fruchtenbaum's *Ariel Ministries* of 1541 Parkway Loop, D Tustin, CA 92680. Particularly recommended is Arnold's definitive book *The Footsteps of the Messiah*. We also recommend Dr. David Reagan's Lamb and Lion Ministries of Texas, PO Box 919, McKinney, TX 75070, website at *www.lamblion.com*, with whom we have had the pleasure of making radio programs and whose books are highly recommended. John Ankerberg's "Facts On" series from Harvest House Publishers of Eugene, Oregon, 97402, was another handy source of reference.

From New Zealand we have drawn on the inspiration of our friend Barry Smith, who alerted us to the stealthy advance of the New World Order in the 1980s on his visits to Britain and his stays with us. His videos and books are available from Barry Smith Family Evangelism, Pelorus Bridge, Rai Valley, Marlborough, New Zealand. Also from New Zealand comes the Christian newsletter *Contending Earnestly for the Faith*, the ministry of Philip Powell; contact via 57, Ruby Street, Levin, 5500, New Zealand.

Christian speakers, broadcasters, and friends have also contributed to this book, knowingly or unknowingly.

Finally, I would like to say a big "thank you" to my wife of twenty-eight years, Patricia Ann, who has humored me as I spent many months working on it, and contributed the best chapter in it—the final chapter which is also her testimony and which you are free to copy and distribute although, of course, the rest of the book is copyrighted.

In whatever spare time I have from editing, writing, and being a husband and father I am available to give illustrated talks to Christian groups in America and Great Britain.

Contact me at

alan.franklin@ntlworld.com